# THE CONFIDENT MANAGER

## LEARN TO MANAGE EFFECTIVELY

### CELESTE CHOA

© Copyright 2022 - All rights reserved.

The content contained within this book may not be reproduced, duplicated or transmitted without direct written permission from the author or the publisher.

Under no circumstances will any blame or legal responsibility be held against the publisher, or author, for any damages, reparation, or monetary loss due to the information contained within this book, either directly or indirectly.

Legal Notice:

This book is copyright protected. It is only for personal use. You cannot amend, distribute, sell, use, quote or paraphrase any part, or the content within this book, without the consent of the author or publisher.

Disclaimer Notice:

Please note the information contained within this document is for educational and entertainment purposes only. All effort has been executed to present accurate, up to date, reliable, complete information. No warranties of any kind are declared or implied. Readers acknowledge that the author is not engaged in the rendering of legal, financial, medical or professional advice. The content within this book has been derived from various sources. Please consult a licensed professional before attempting any techniques outlined in this book.

By reading this document, the reader agrees that under no circumstances is the author responsible for any losses, direct or indirect, that are incurred as a result of the use of the information contained within this document, including, but not limited to, errors, omissions, or inaccuracies.

# CONTENTS

| | |
|---|---|
| *Introduction* | vii |
| 1. UNDERSTANDING MANAGEMENT | 1 |
| Leadership vs Management | 2 |
| What Do Managers do? | 4 |
| What Do Leaders do? | 5 |
| Characteristics of an Effective Manager | 6 |
| 2. SELF-MANAGEMENT | 11 |
| Improving Self-Management Skills | 14 |
| Workplace Self-Management Skills | 16 |
| 3. MANAGING OTHERS | 19 |
| What Every First-Time Manager Should Know | 19 |
| Styles of Management | 26 |
| How to Manage People | 30 |
| Mistakes That First-Time Managers Should Avoid | 36 |
| 4. DELEGATING WORK | 41 |
| Strategies for Effective Delegation | 42 |
| How to Delegate Duties | 45 |
| Types of Delegation | 47 |
| Dos and Don'ts of Delegating | 49 |
| 5. GOAL-SETTING | 53 |
| The Benefits of Setting Goals | 54 |
| What Are Smart Goals? | 55 |
| Goal-Setting Mistakes | 58 |
| 6. DIVERSITY AND INCLUSION | 61 |
| Challenges of Leading Diverse Teams | 62 |
| What Makes a Leader Inclusive? | 63 |
| Competencies to Improve When Managing Diverse Teams | 64 |
| Overcoming Challenges of Workplace Diversity | 69 |
| The Benefits of a Diverse Workforce | 70 |

| | |
|---|---|
| 7. PURPOSE | 75 |
| Leadership and Purpose | 76 |
| 8. CONFLICT RESOLUTION | 91 |
| Causes of Conflict in the Workplace | 92 |
| Levels of Conflict | 94 |
| Signs of Conflict in the Team | 100 |
| How to Resolve Conflict in the Workplace | 101 |
| 9. STRATEGIC PLANNING AND IMPLEMENTATION | 107 |
| Process of Strategic Planning | 107 |
| Strategy Implementation | 113 |
| 10. SETTING KEY PERFORMANCE INDICATORS | 119 |
| Choosing the Right KPIs | 122 |
| Implementing KPIs Effectively | 123 |
| Developing SMART KPIs | 124 |
| 11. MANAGING CHANGE | 127 |
| Change Management Levels | 128 |
| Types of Organizational Change | 129 |
| Managing Change | 130 |
| Change Management Mistakes to Avoid | 133 |
| *Conclusion* | 137 |
| *References* | 141 |
| *About the Author* | 147 |

*This book is dedicated to my family who have been my rock from start to finish of this project. I could not have done this without my husband keeping me on tract and my kids being patient with me when I needed protected time.*

# INTRODUCTION

You've just recently been promoted to your first managerial position. It is such an incredible opportunity, congratulations on your achievement!

You were an exceptional employee because of your hard work, performance, and commitment, but now you must manage a team. Rather than relying on yourself, you'll need to work with and through your team to achieve goals by prioritizing, organizing, and delegating duties. You must convey strategic and team goals while also ensuring that your team's deliverables are completed.

With your new job comes a slew of new responsibilities. As a manager, you are a coach, conductor, teacher, scientist, and psychologist. Like most new managers, you'll need to simultaneously perform these things while also working toward accomplishing your own deliverables. Correction—like *all* managers.

Of course, you're still employed by the organization. You are an employee. However, you are no longer an isolated performer—your success will now be assessed mostly by how your team members perform on their deliverables. This definitely appears to be a lot— and it is! And there is no alternative for on-the-job training.

INTRODUCTION

However, you may make your work a lot simpler by educating yourself as you go.

When the excitement of your promotion finally dissipates, your mind gets flooded with thousands of questions about this new role. Some of the questions might include:

- How do I manage a team?
- How do I delegate tasks?
- What do I do with team members who are not performing?
- What happens if there's a conflict?
- What if I make mistakes?
- Is this new position anything like my last job?
- What if I'm not as good as the last manager?

Whoa! Stop! Breathe…

Great managers learn how to be great on the job. Fortunately, you have this book to help you maneuver your way through the managerial position maze. In this book, you will find information that will empower you to be the best manager you can be while leading your team members to be the best they can be in their various roles.

This is meant to be used as a reference as you get along with your job. It is not something you can read in one sitting and put away. The content in this book is most effective if you engage with it and put it to practice. The purpose of this book is to teach you the following:

- how to manage and lead your team confidently
- how to delegate effectively
- how to deal with workplace conflicts successfully
- the ins and outs of strategic planning and implementation

- how to handle conflict resolution efficiently
- how tell help your team through change

This book is a guide. After reading each chapter, you should be able to put what you've learned into practice. By the end of the book, you will be able to do the following:

- Know how to sync your management style with that of the individuals in your team.
- Lead an inclusive and diverse team with confidence.
- Trust your abilities as a manager.
- Know how to properly harness the strengths of each member of your team.
- Lead your team purposefully.
- Inspire your team members to take on bigger responsibilities.
- Lead a team that understands how their jobs impact the overall success of the organization.
- Set KPI that are aligned to organizational goals.
- Confidently set attainable and measurable goals for your team.

My hope is for you to use this book as your constant companion throughout your first year in your managerial position and use it going forward in your career to refresh your knowledge. Every time you read this book, you should find information and content that helps you learn and grow.

1

# UNDERSTANDING MANAGEMENT

You cannot talk about management without talking about leadership. It is important that we first address the difference between management and leadership. These two concepts are commonly used interchangeably, but that's a mistake, because they are not the same.

First, let's talk about what management is.

Management entails carrying out pre-planned duties on a regular basis with the assistance of subordinates. A manager is solely responsible for carrying out the four essential management activities of organizing, planning, controlling, and leading. Managers can only become leaders if they carry out their leadership tasks effectively, which include communicating both good and bad news, offering inspiration and advice, and motivating people to achieve better levels of productivity. Unfortunately, not all managers are capable of doing so. Managerial duties are frequently described in a job description, with subordinates trailing behind due to the professional title or classification. A manager's major focus is on attaining organizational goals; they rarely consider anything else. The ability and privilege to promote, hire, or reward personnel based on their performance and conduct comes with the title.

Leadership, on the other hand, is the process of bringing about constructive, non-incremental change by careful preparation, vision, and strategy. The ability to empower people and adaptable decision-making are also important leadership characteristics. People frequently associate leadership with one's position in an organization; however, titles, personal agendas, or positions have nothing to do with leadership. It also has little to do with personality attributes such as charm and ambition. It is an exercise in social influence where an individual has the ability to influence others to perform at their best to achieve a common objective or goal. A leader is someone who constantly takes the initiative and works hard to achieve the organization's objective. That is the sole reason why others begin to follow them.

Let's take a closer look at the differences.

## LEADERSHIP VS MANAGEMENT

It is possible to be both a manager and a leader. However, just because someone is a terrific leader doesn't automatically mean they will be a great manager. A leader is continually looking ahead, inventing new approaches and plans for the organization. A leader is well-versed in all current trends, innovations, and skill sets, as well as having a clear purpose and goal. A manager, on the other hand, typically merely maintains what has already been built. A manager must watch the bottom line while avoiding chaos and managing employees and workflow in the organization.

Alan Murray defines a manager as someone who "establishes appropriate targets and yardsticks, and analyzes, appraises, and interprets performance" in his book, *The Wall Street Journal Essential Guide to Management: Lasting Lessons from the Best Leadership Minds of*

*Our Time* (2010). Managers understand the people they work with and know which person is the best fit for a specific task.

So, what criteria separate these two roles?

### 1. Difference in focus and vision

Leaders are often regarded as visionaries. They chart the course for the organization's expansion. They are always assessing where their organization is, where they want to go, and how they might get there by incorporating the team.

Managers, on the other hand, set out to achieve corporate goals by executing processes like budgeting, personnel, and organizational architecture. Managers' visions are linked to implementation techniques, planning, and coordinating work to achieve their goals. However, in commercial contexts, each of these responsibilities are equally significant and demand collaborative efforts.

### 2. Alignment vs Organization

Managers attain their objectives through the use of coordinated actions and tactical processes. They break down long-term goals into little chunks and organize available resources to achieve the desired result.

Leaders, on the other hand, are more concerned with how to align and influence people than on assigning tasks. They accomplish this by supporting individuals in visualizing their roles in a larger context and the potential for future growth that their efforts may bring forth.

### 3. Difference in what they inquire about

A leader inquires about what and why, whereas a manager inquires about how and when. To fulfill their obligations as a leader, she may question and challenge authority to reverse actions that are not in the best interests of the team. If an organization encounters a stumbling block, a leader will be the one to stand up and ask, "What did we learn from this?" and "Why has this occurred?"

Managers, on the other hand, are not compelled to examine and analyze failures. Their job is to ask 'How?' and 'When?', which helps them ensure that plans are carried out appropriately. They would rather accept the status quo than try to alter it.

**4. Quality vs Position**

A manager is a role that often refers to a function within the structure of an organization, whereas the word 'leader' is more vague. Your behaviors determine your level of leadership. You are a leader if your actions motivate others to perform their best. It doesn't matter what your title or position is. A manager, on the other hand, is a job title that comes with a set of responsibilities.

WHAT DO MANAGERS DO?

A manager is in charge of carrying out the four fundamental management functions:

- planning
- organizing
- leading
- controlling

Are all managers leaders?
Most managers are also leaders, but this can be the case only if they properly carry out management's leadership tasks, which include communication, encouragement, being inspirational,

giving direction, and motivating people to increase their productivity.

But, not all managers are leaders. Some managers have inadequate leadership skills, and employees obey their bosses out of obligation rather than because they are persuaded or inspired by the leader. Managerial responsibilities are often outlined in a job description, with subordinates following as a result of the professional title or classification. A manager's primary emphasis is on meeting organizational goals and objectives; they often do not consider anything else. Managers are held accountable for their acts as well as those of their subordinates. Remember that the authority and privilege to promote, appoint, dismiss, reprimand, or reward workers depending on their performance and conduct come with the position.

## WHAT DO LEADERS DO?

The main distinction between management and leadership is that leaders do not always have or occupy a management job. Simply defined, a leader does not have to be someone in a position of authority inside the business; a leader can be anyone. What makes people follow leaders is their behavior, personality, and beliefs. A leader personally invests in tasks and projects and demonstrates a strong work ethic. Leaders are deeply invested in the success of their followers, allowing them to achieve their objectives—which are not always corporate objectives.

A leader's authority over his followers is not necessarily physical or official. Temporary authority is granted to a leader and might be conditional on the leader's capacity to consistently inspire and encourage their supporters.

When it comes to leadership, subordinates are obligated to obey commands; however, following is voluntary. Leadership relies on employee motivation and trust—those who desire to follow their leader may do so at any time. Leaders, in general, are those who question the existing state of affairs. Leadership is flexible, imaginative, nimble, creative, and adaptable.

## CHARACTERISTICS OF AN EFFECTIVE MANAGER

You may be pursuing your next professional objective of becoming a manager. You're waiting for your boss to come around the corner with an offer for your next great adventure—running your own team. Perhaps you are on the other end of the spectrum, a manager looking to improve your leadership style. Being a manager is difficult.

As a manager, you are in charge of an organization's most valuable asset: its people. Consider this. Regardless of how much the world tries to push artificial intelligence in the workplace, businesses cannot function without the expertise of human intelligence.

There is no step-by-step roadmap to being an effective manager. Every team, organization, and sector has a unique structure and culture. Not only do you need a great team, but you also need a strong leader to steer them in the proper way. Managers are in charge of everything, from hiring the right people to managing work methods, procedures, and regulations.

Keep in mind that people do not leave their organizations; they leave their managers.

So, what are the qualities of an effective manager?

Managers are not given the opportunity to lead their own team out of nowhere; they have to work for it. Whether it was demonstrating their sector competence through self-study or training supplied through their existing work. In any case, they have earned their place and have consistently exceeded expectations.

## Expertise from experience

Managers often have years of expertise in the field they are heading. Through those experiences, they have gone above and beyond, learning from both the good and the terrible. Most importantly, great managers have invested the time required to learn this area and understand exactly how to accomplish targets month after month.

## Communication

Communication is essential in all relationships, but especially between people who work together every day. Communicate objectives, expectations, and any resources your team may require to accomplish those expectations effectively. Listen to what your team is dealing with and how to properly devote time and learning to overcome that development hurdle. Clear communication is important for more than simply making all employees feel appreciated; it also helps to improve efficiency. Beyond talking, excellent managers incorporate clarity principles throughout every process, from staff onboarding to operations.

## Reliability

As a manager, you are the initial point of contact for every employee you supervise. Making yourself available for any queries or concerns that your team may have is critical to their growth and success. Demonstrate that you are trustworthy, honest, and appreciative of your and your team's time while putting out flames and celebrating outstanding accomplishments.

**Time management**

Managers plan their time and the time of others around projected goals. When it comes to reducing stress on your team, it is critical to ensure that you are allowing adequate time to properly complete tasks and any other thing that may need to be completed. Set reasonable weekly, monthly, quarterly, and annual goals, and watch for signs that your staff is more stressed than usual.

**Organization**

Managers who have the ability to combine their communication and time management abilities to create clear expectations may successfully put goals into action. Organize simple actions that might help your team reach big goals without putting them under stress. The greatest managers have regular meetings to convey what is required and to keep every member on task and prepared to fulfill their goals.

**Empathy**

Ethical management entails empathizing with your employees. When you understand your people, you can pull the best out of them. One of the most highly desired job characteristics is empathy. Even in the most compassionate communities, though, stress and targets can impair our ability to empathize. This implies you should take a step back and consider what your staff want and need. If you are unsure what their thoughts are, have a meeting and ask them.

**Diplomacy**

Of course, there are unpleasant parts of managing. If your team is experiencing performance challenges, unpleasant talks may be required. Your team expects and deserves for you to handle the difficult stuff. This is due to the fact that failing to address poor performance can be demotivating for high-performing staff.

Seek out a secluded meeting space for difficult topics. Make sure you're in the correct frame of mind, and if things get tough, take a 10- or 20-minute break. It is critical to be explicit in your messaging: If a particular behavior is wrong, state so.

## The ability to 'read' situations and people

Great managers can read people—their employees, business partners, and external connections. This enables them to comprehend what inspires workers and to communicate effectively. Effective managers have emotional intelligence, especially when it comes to workplace mental health. Paying attention to sentiments may help to establish a good environment, which leads to increased productivity.

You may need to personalize efforts to each employee based on their personality and role on the team. If you have a stagnate employee, for example, a 'coaching' or 'challenging' strategy may be suited to unleash their potential.

## Leadership

Managers are constantly guiding and responding to any issues or conflicts that emerge. Every day, successful leaders encourage people to be the greatest version of themselves at work. They are thinking strategically about the broad picture and how to proactively achieve their team's next set of goals. When it comes to showcasing and enabling development and cooperation on your team, being a smart leader is essential.

2

# SELF-MANAGEMENT

Every manager's toolkit should include a set of self-management abilities. Change is a new reality, and managers must adapt and manage their teams in real time. The work environment is evolving faster than ever before.

Let's define self-management in the workplace before we get into the important self-management abilities that managers should have. Self-management is a set of behaviors that govern how you manage yourself at work. These behaviors enable you to increase your working performance, enhance your productivity, and reach professional goals more efficiently. Improving your self-management abilities can help you boost your employability and manage your professional path more effectively.

As a manager, it's important that you continuously learn and grow in order to effectively manage your staff. However, managing oneself is a full-time job. It's something you need to master. Are you capable of cultivating and motivating your team while also motivating yourself to discover new things? A self-managed manager is a productive manager.

Consider these self-management skills that every manager should acquire in order to be as effective as possible in their position:

**Organization**

Being organized enables you to plan, prioritize, and execute important activities, helping you effectively manage your critical workplace responsibilities. You can apply your organizational skills across all aspects of your job—your physical space, time, mental capabilities, and energy to improve functionality.

**Stress management**

Stress has the potential to kill you. Every day, a manager's work entails dealing with challenging situations. Stress management strategies can help you navigate and handle the diversity of events that arise on a daily basis. Delaying the initial reaction is one of the easiest things a manager can do to assist with managing stress in certain situations. Take a deep breath and consider an effective solution to the situation. This introspection will put you in the optimal mental frame to make informed judgments.

**Time management**

As a manager, you are well aware that time does not wait for anybody. You must balance various duties at all times. You will fail if you do not plan ahead of time. Prioritizing is the first step in mastering your time management abilities. Make a list of everything that has to be done. After examining the list, begin to eliminate any redundant chores or tasks. Take advantage of all available resources to complete your job list. Recognize your coworkers' skill sets and distribute duties where necessary. Remember to always convey your plan and approach to all parties involved. Time management enables you to create a structure for productivity and effectiveness.

**Holding yourself accountable**

Accountability is being able to take personal ownership of your actions and thoughts. When you maintain responsibility, you're better equipped to look at your work, assess it accordingly, and determine the best way to proceed.

**Knowing when to delegate**

Your time is precious in the office, and attempting to do too many activities at once might result in burnout and unneeded stress. By delegating non-essential duties to others, you may focus on your main abilities and responsibilities.

**Decision-making**

Making decisions is a necessary skill that fosters operational excellence. As a manager, you are likely to make critical decisions that impact your organization's strategy. This ability necessitates trust in your judgment. Your decisions should be objective and not based on emotions or conflicts of interest. It's important to get feedback from coworkers, but be wary of "too many cooks in the kitchen." When making your final decision, stick to the facts and be confident.

Being able to manage your time effectively can help you avoid procrastination as well as ensure that you stay engaged. As a leader, time management allows you to stay on top of your own work while also empowering others to do the same.

## Problem-solving

When confronted with a challenging problem, a manager must be brave. You may encounter technical or interpersonal issues. The primary takeaway is to maintain objectivity. First, comprehend the issue. Second, determine what is causing the issue. Third, inquire as to what may be done to address the issue. Finally, decide which approach is appropriate for your organization and what steps must be made to discover a solution.

## Motivating yourself

Self-motivation is the ability to take the initiative and complete tasks that you know should be done. When you are self-motivated, you anticipate and plan for potential tasks that will be required to complete larger assignments or resolve ongoing issues. You are motivated by your desire to succeed rather than by external factors, which makes you more productive at work. Self-motivation is the aspect of self-management that ensures that your projects and activities move forward.

### IMPROVING SELF-MANAGEMENT SKILLS

Improve your self-management skills by focusing on how you can direct, evaluate, and improve your daily tasks. Here are a few suggestions to help you improve your self-management abilities:

## Evaluate your abilities

Determine which work-specific tasks you excel at and work on ways to improve your performance in these areas. Understanding your strengths allows you to manage your career path in a way that maximizes skills, such as technical writing, coding, customer service, and graphic design.

**Rank your responsibilities in order of importance**

Define which responsibilities are the most important and focus your attention on those tasks, avoiding distractions that take you away from completing them.

**Create systems to help keep you organized**

Find efficient methods for streamlining your daily activities, managing your time, and keeping important items where you can easily access them. This could include installing a time-management app on your phone, creating an agenda book, or establishing a filing system at your desk.

**Establish deadlines and adhere to them**

Maintain your schedule by assigning deadlines to each stage of a project. Hold yourself accountable for completing tasks on time or ahead of schedule by committing to working extra hours when necessary to meet your self-defined checkpoints.

**Avoid multitasking**

At any given time, concentrate your time, abilities, and energy on a single task. Complete each task completely before moving on to the next so that you can manage your time effectively and finish each task efficiently.

### Exercise patience

Maintain your calm so that you can think clearly and objectively. Consider others and try to empathize with their needs and experiences in order to help them more effectively.

### Take good care of your health and well-being

Exercise regularly and maintain a healthy diet, take care of your personal hygiene, and actively work to reduce your stress levels. Take breaks to clear your mind and stretch, keep healthy snacks on hand at work, and maximize opportunities for movement or physical activity. Guard against sitting at your desk the whole day and take brisk walks during your lunch break.

### Examine and monitor your progress

Set checkpoints along the way and track your accomplishments to see if you've met them to objectively assess your progress toward your goals. To obtain a well-rounded evaluation, seek the assistance of a mentor. Use this feedback to help you improve your self-management in the future.

## WORKPLACE SELF-MANAGEMENT SKILLS

Managing your workplace activities carefully can help you effectively achieve work objectives. Use the following suggestions to practice self-management at work and keep an efficient and productive schedule:

**Always be punctual and fully prepared for meetings**

If you know you'll be attending a meeting, the day before the meeting spend some time gathering any information you'll need and familiarize yourself with it. You can also use this time to write down questions you'll need clarity on. An hour before you go into the meeting, review your questions and notes to ensure you are focused on the meeting's objectives and can contribute collaboratively.

**At the end of each work day, make plans for the next day**

At the end of each workday, set aside time to go through your calendar, organize your planner to include tasks that should be undertaken the next day, or to create a list of things that should be attended to. Furthermore, use these last hours of your work day to reflect on what you accomplished for the day and whether you succeeded in meeting your daily objectives.

**Maintain an organized calendar**

You can create a schedule of deadlines, events, and meetings to help you manage your tasks, projects, and responsibilities better. A task-tracking app or a planner will help keep you organized.

**Outline the project's objectives**

Set firm deadlines and track them regularly—it could be daily, weekly, monthly, and quarterly. Use a calendar with reminders to help keep on top of things.

**Early project evaluation**

Before you begin a project, prepare a list of questions to ensure you understand your role. This exercise of asking yourself questions can also be undertaken after starting a task to ensure that you are completing it correctly or to determine if you need to make any changes.

3

# MANAGING OTHERS

To manage others, you must first commit to improving and developing your leadership skills and qualities. Good managers can adapt their leadership styles to different personalities in the workplace, incorporating feedback from their surroundings to achieve goals. To effectively manage others, you must first identify what motivates different people and then find ways to emphasize those motivating factors in various situations. It also entails mediating conflicts among team members and employing problem-solving techniques to promote a productive environment.

WHAT EVERY FIRST-TIME MANAGER SHOULD KNOW

Managers set the tone for the work experience; they are the organizational cultural linchpins. You can work for a fantastic organization, but if your manager isn't up to par, it will overshadow everything else. There's truth in the phrase "People don't leave their jobs, they leave their managers."

To get started, here are 10 tips to create a work environment in which your team will thrive and help you get the most out of them.

## 1. Being a manager means you're not an individual contributor

Being a manager is a completely different game from being a regular worker; playing by the old rules rather than adapting to the new rules will only lead to failure for you and your team.

You most likely did not rise to the position of manager because you demonstrated your ability to manage a group of individual contributors. You got this position because you demonstrated your ability to succeed as an individual contributor. These are two different roles. You can't wake up one day knowing what to do to be the world's best manager if you've never managed people. It's a skill that, like any other, must be developed. So, as a first-time manager, consider yourself in training.

Your first position as a manager is the time to learn how to take on the leadership role that your team requires, how to inspire your team to give their all every day, and how to delegate effectively. Own the mistakes you make along the way and make a real effort to not repeat those mistakes and do better next time.

## 2. People are more comfortable when there's structure

A few years ago, online shoe and retailer Zappos made headlines when they transitioned to a holacracy and effectively eliminated manager positions. This did not end well, with 18% of their workforce leaving the company (Guzman, 2016).

The idea of allowing lower-level employees to be more entrepreneurial and removing managers looks great on paper, but in practice it rarely works because most people seek structure and guidance from a psychological standpoint. This is how we've been conditioned from childhood. You can't turn off over 20 years of programming when you enter the workforce—people expect constant feedback.

Someone must provide guidance, and simply stating that it is everyone's responsibility is not sufficient. When everyone is responsible for something, it is really no one's responsibility. As a result, it is up to managers to do it. In fact, according to research conducted by employee engagement firm OfficeVibe, 65% of people say they want more feedback from their managers than they currently receive (2016). Your job as a manager is to ensure that there's structure so your team members can do their best work on a consistent basis.

### 3. Structure should not be rigid

Managers must walk a fine line between providing guidance and micromanaging. Here are some key distinctions between managers who micromanage and effective managers:

- Effective managers do not lead through control, they lead through influence. Micromanaging is the need to control and not based on influence.
- Effective managers understand that the occasional failure is the only way to learn and grow. Micromanagers are terrified of any type of failure, no matter how insignificant.
- Effective managers ask questions that lead their teams to a solution. Micromanagers impose a solution without considering alternative options or opportunities.
- Effective managers empower their team members by not interfering; all they require is updates and will provide assistance when necessary. Micromanagers must be present at every meeting and copied on every email.
- Effective managers always play open cards. They openly and transparently share information. Micromanagers

play their cards close to their chest and monopolize information.
- Effective managers are open to new ideas and ways of doing things and are willing to investigate them if they appear reasonable. Micromanagers tend to do things the same way they've always done them.

As a manager, it is your responsibility to ensure that your team members have the tools to do their work as best they can so they can learn and grow. Your job is not to stifle or control their growth.

**4. Adaptation is your panacea**

If you want your team members to be highly productive, creative, motivated, and innovative—you must learn to adapt your working style to theirs.

Everyone you manage will have a different work rhythm and style of work, and this means they will all have different things that will motivate and inspire them, as well as things that will make it difficult for them to do their best work. On occasion, you will have employees whose working style syncs with yours, and you gel right away. Most times your style of work will differ vastly from that of the individuals in your team. It's important to remember that each work style has its own merits and that no work style is superior or inferior to any other.

In an ideal world, we would all understand our colleagues' work styles and do everything we can to adapt and meet somewhere in the middle. As a manager, it is your responsibility, if you want to help your team perform at their best, to work to understand their needs and adapt your work style to them. Remember, their success is your success.

## 5. Allow your employees to take the lead on their projects and in their areas

It's important to take a step back to allow your employees to do their best work. Your role is to provide guidance, which you can do by asking questions to ensure that your team member has thoroughly weighed their approach. However, if their ideas differ from how you would have done it, most of the time it is best to let them try what they want and see what happens. There is always more than one way to accomplish something. If they do not succeed, take it as a learning experience and an opportunity to iterate. And even if they win using a strategy you wouldn't have chosen, it's still a win for you and your team.

## 6. Schedule one-on-one meetings on a regular and frequent basis

Few people want to attend more meetings, but for managers, a weekly one-on-one meeting with each direct report is a must.

Yes, I did say weekly. Consider this: If you can't devote 30 minutes per week to each of your direct reports, you either have too many people reporting to you (and need to add more hierarchy), or you haven't fully embraced your role as a manager rather than an individual contributor.

You want to cover three topics in those one-on-one meetings:

- their update on what they've been working on, the challenges they've experienced, and what they need from you to help them succeed
- your update to them on everything they need to know to do their job well, including new information or insight.

- a quick brainstorm of future goals, ideas, and development that may be required (This is also an excellent place to incorporate coaching.)

One-on-one meetings are frequently the first to be canceled with people, saying they have nothing to report back. You should not cancel your one-on-one meetings unless there's a crisis or something urgent which makes having the meeting impossible. These meetings are important for developing a trusting relationship with each of your employees. It's one of the most crucial things you can do to help their projects succeed, and in turn, them.

**7. Make trust a default setting and listen actively**

When you have your weekly one-on-one meetings, the most important aspect is not what you say but what your team members contribute to it. Be prepared to hear both the good and the bad, because that's bound to happen when people communicate openly. It is critical that you listen to your employees and always assume they are coming to you with good intentions. They are complaining about problems because they want your assistance in solving them. Be open and trust their intentions and motivations.

You should ensure that at the end of the one-on-one meeting, they leave feeling better about their work and more empowered than when they arrived. Pay close attention to their requests, read between the lines to get to the bottom of their issues and challenges, and then do all you can to provide the assistance they require.

**8. Never give negative emotional feedback; concentrate on behavior and impact**

When you work with people, you can't completely eliminate

the role of emotions in the workplace, but that doesn't mean you have to comment on them. When all is said and done, people can think or feel whatever they want as long as they show up and do what they need to do to achieve their goals. That is why, when providing feedback, it is critical to concentrate on what you can see in terms of their work. Your goal is to change someone's behavior and get them to stop doing something that isn't working and instead explore something different. To do so, you must be completely clear about what they are doing and why there should be adjustments.

Identify the problematic behavior, explain why it is problematic, and establish the expectation for future behavior. Then move on to the next point, thank them for a job well done, and provide positive feedback when they meet or exceed expectations.

### 9. Be unapologetic in your optimism

It is important that you provide far more positive feedback than negative feedback, because positive feedback is far more motivating than critical feedback (Burgers et al., 2015). When your brain is in a positive state, every single business outcome that can be measured improves.

And the truth is, most employees do the majority of their work properly on any given day, but they only receive feedback when they do something incorrectly. The manner in which you provide feedback will set the tone for your management style. If you're constantly seeking reasons to praise your team, even for the smallest things, you'll keep them in the right frame of mind, and they'll be inclined to do better to keep the praises coming.

## 10. It is your responsibility to ensure the success of your employees

You will be evaluated based on how successful your team is at delivering on organizational objectives. This means your team is your top priority.

It may be beneficial to perform a quick exercise at the end of each day and make a list of the ways that you set your team members up for success that day. It will assist you in taking stock, holding yourself accountable, and ensuring that you are focusing on the most important things.

### STYLES OF MANAGEMENT

Your organization, the people you manage, and your objectives will determine your management style. As mentioned earlier in this chapter, you need to adapt your work style to sync with that of the individuals in your team.

Each style of management has advantages and disadvantages; there is no one-size-fits-all style that will work in every scenario. Instead, you must identify your temperament, character qualities, and the sorts of people you have in your team in order to determine the best management technique.

Your management style tells others how you plan, make decisions, organize your work, and exercise authority. Depending on the circumstances, you may employ a range of management styles in your working life.

Effective managers do not use just one style of management, they use different styles of management depending on their goals or circumstances they are dealing with. To determine which management style to use, they may look at the following aspects:

- amount of work to be completed and deadlines
- their abilities as leaders
- organizational culture and industry
- their team and organizational objectives
- the attitudes and characteristics of their team members

Let's discuss seven types of the most common management styles for effective leadership, as well as their benefits and drawbacks and how you can develop your unique management style.

**1. Dominant Style of Management**

This manager is authoritative and approaches leadership from the top down. Managers who use this style of management make decisions on their own and do not consult their teams fully on their own. They establish strict and detailed regulations that everyone must obey, and they rarely solicit employee opinion.

This approach is excellent when efficiency is crucial, as well as in crisis circumstances where effective judgments must be made swiftly. However, it doesn't allow for innovation and new ways of doing things. When used incorrectly, it can lead to an increase in staff turnover.

**2. Consultative Style of Management**

Consultative managers solicit input from team members on a regular basis and take employee issues seriously. They frequently have an open-door policy, which encourages people to express what works and what doesn't on their projects and in the organization. While managers will confer with staff, they will ultimately have the final say.

This management approach frequently results in stronger team problem-solving, increased employee engagement, and lower turnover. However, when many individuals are engaged in decision-making, things do not run as smoothly and efficiently.

### 3. Participatory Style of Management

The decision-making process of participatory management is highly impacted by their staff. This approach incorporates transparency and good communication at all levels of the business. Managers and employees are required to collaborate to achieve the set goals. Participatory management is highly successful when making long-term decisions that affect the whole organization.

A participatory management style makes employees feel valued and empowered to make substantial contributions. It also inspires them to work to their greatest ability.

This style of management can be inefficient because at times, decision-making turns into lengthy arguments and drawn-out consultations with various stakeholders.

### 4. Persuasive Management Style

Persuasive managers have power over decision-making but seek to assist people comprehend why those decisions will benefit the organization at large. They give an open explanation for policy decisions that can build an inclusive and trustworthy workplace. Employees tend to accept top-down decisions if the organization they work for is successful.

This management style inspires and informs employees by reason and reasoning, which some people prefer over authoritative management. It is very useful when leading a team with less expertise. However, persuasive management is a one-way communication process in which employees do not always have an opportunity to provide feedback.

### 5. Laissez-faire Management Style

Managers who use the laissez-faire management style act more like mentors than leaders. They are accessible for help when needed, but they frequently let staff make their own judgments on how to proceed with tasks. Managers with this management style keep an eye on what's going on with their staff but don't become too engaged in day-to-day duties or initiatives.

The laissez-faire management style provides self-motivated individuals with the liberty and space they require to be productive. This might be very valuable in a creative setting. However, because this management style is hands-off, employees who need more advice and direction to deliver may feel ignored.

### 6. Collaborative Style of Management

Collaborative leaders collaborate extensively with their team members because they think that when individuals are personally and professionally happy, they are more successful and more likely to do exceptional work on a consistent basis. They tend to acquire higher levels of respect due to their emphasis on employee happiness and collaboration.

A collaborative style of management is great for businesses of any size or sector but is particularly common in non-governmental organizations (NGOs). These managers are great at boosting employee morale and re-engaging employees in their job. Collaborative managers may increase staff loyalty and productivity, promote employee growth and decision-making, foster trust, and produce future leaders. They are also more knowledgeable about the difficulties of getting things done on their team. However, these managers might burn out as they try to increase cooperation with and among their team members. They may also struggle to find time for strategic planning at a higher level.

### 7. Transformational Style of Management

A manager who practices a transformational style of management is all about establishing an atmosphere that allows and enables creativity. Leaders using this approach frequently push their people out of their comfort zones; they encourage them to create and achieve goals. These managers work closely with their team members and motivate them to meet their full potential and strive for professional excellence. This management style often increases adaptability, problem-solving, and creativity. It can be especially beneficial for businesses in competitive industries that change rapidly. However, this management approach will not work for everyone. Some team members may be unwilling to adopt top-down ideas if they are not ready to adapt or if they feel overwhelmed by the rush of changes.

HOW TO MANAGE PEOPLE

As discussed in the previous chapter, before you can manage others successfully, you need to take care of yourself. Make your own schedule a priority and guard your time by allocating a block of time each day to complete your own work without interruptions. Eager managers may make the mistake of overcommitting to their team, resulting in burnout, making them a less effective manager. When you are confident in your own work, you will be able to pay more attention to and focus on your team when they require it.

**Know Your Team**

Understanding the people you manage is the first step toward effective management. People react differently to different leadership styles depending on their personality type. Some people need hands-on management, while others thrive when given freedom and flexibility. Strong leaders can adapt their management techniques based on who they are working with, cultivating each team member's individual potential with personalized attention.

Learning what inspires your team, how they approach their work, factors that hinder or support their productivity within the work environment, and the level of knowledge and skills they bring to their work are all part of getting to know them. Knowing how someone works best and evaluating their competency in various areas can help you assign tasks effectively and address issues in the most productive way possible without lowering morale. You can start learning about your team by engaging in conversation with active listening skills.

This is particularly important for delegation purposes, as you'll need to match responsibilities to skill sets. You'll need to know what each team member excels at and what work atmosphere or style of management works best for them. This will also help you determine where they may benefit from more development and ensure that any training or resources your team requires to accomplish their portion of the project are available.

**Delegate Work**

Learning to delegate crucial activities to others helps you to focus on high-level management obligations rather than micromanaging each duty on a project. You will be able to correctly delegate duties to the people who are likely to accomplish them well within the specified time period once you have learned about each team member's strengths, limitations, experiences, and talents. Setting clear expectations with each individual and guaranteeing their confidence in their capacity to fulfill their component of the project are all part of delegating assignments. Delegating responsibility to others demonstrates faith in their talents and helps them feel engaged in the result of a project.

Delegating work will be discussed in depth in Chapter 4.

**Initiate Communication**

Instead of waiting for members of your team to contact you with questions, updates, and concerns, be proactive and intimate communication—don't wait for them to come to you. Let your team members know how they should communicate with you and one another as soon as you assume your managerial role, whether unofficial or official. Identify the primary communication channels, such as email or chat servers, so that everyone knows what to do if an issue arises. Check in with your team, both as a group and individually, to see how they're doing and to foster open communication as a way to solve problems.

**Determine Distinct Workflows**

Identify each team member's role in project completion and map out the workflow processes you intend to use. Understanding each individual role and how it affects the overall project gives you a better idea of what you can expect from each person. It also allows you to create a reasonable timeline that employees can follow. Managing employees without understanding the project workflow can lead to confusion and delays, making it difficult to identify the root cause of any problems that arise.

**Set Specific Goals**

Set team and individual goals to guide your management efforts. Developing goals at the start of a project keeps everyone focused on their tasks and provides you, as a leader, with a guideline to affect the success of a project or initiative. Write down each goal so you have a document to refer to when evaluating project success at key milestones. Discuss with your team the steps that everyone needs to take to achieve their goals, giving everyone the opportunity to ask questions and make suggestions on how to meet or exceed team goals.

When creating goals, consider using the SMART method so that you have a clear way of determining whether your team has met their goals or not. SMART stands for specific, measurable, achievable, relevant, and time-bound. This means that each goal you set must have specific guidelines and a method for tracking progress on a regular basis. Goals that adhere to the SMART framework are simple to manage because they are tailored to each team member's specific role and include metrics that hold everyone accountable.

**Be Consistent in Your Leadership**

Being a good manager requires you to build trust within your team. Being consistent in your behavior is one of the best ways to demonstrate your trustworthiness and earn the respect of others. When you say you're going to do something, always follow through. Although you should tailor your management techniques to each individual, you must also hold everyone to the same behavioral standards in order to avoid showing favoritism. Consistent, dependable follow-through demonstrates to your team that they can rely on you to be fair and equitable with everyone involved in a project.

**Use Positive Reinforcement**

Positive reinforcement is a highly effective management technique that rewards employees who excel in the workplace. When you notice someone doing quality work, speak up and encourage team members to celebrate one another's success. Depending on what motivates your team the most, you can recognize excellent work with something as simple as verbal praise or through a structured reward system. Find something positive to highlight about each member of your team so that you can recognize top performers and encourage others to be more confident as they develop their skills.

**Provide Truthful Feedback**

When giving both praise and constructive criticism to their team, good managers can be tactful and direct. To get the most out of others, you must be able to be honest about their strengths and weaknesses, recognizing when their work falls short of expectations and strategizing on how to improve. Your feedback should be honest but not discouraging so that failures can be used as opportunities for growth rather than demoralizing moments.

**Actively Settle Disagreements**

While maintaining a professional connection with each member of your team is essential for management, you should also be aware of how team members communicate with one another. Interpersonal or professional disagreements among team members can stymie output and lead to miscommunications throughout the organization. If you identify a disagreement, take efforts to mediate and actively address it before it becomes a widespread problem that disrupts workflow. Conflict resolution is covered at length in Chapter 6.

## Solicit Feedback

Just as it is crucial that you provide clear, constructive criticism to your team, it is also critical that you seek input on your management abilities. Allow your employees to share their experiences and make comments on how you can be a better manager and provide the support they require to succeed. When you hear feedback from your team, thank them for their ideas and thoroughly evaluate how you may remedy the issues they raised.

Consider using an anonymous channel so that everyone may express themselves without fear of embarrassment or retaliation, especially if you have seniority over your team members. Their comments might assist you in adjusting individual workloads to avoid burnout, changing unhelpful business rules, or reorganizing the process to increase efficiency.

## Allow for Some Leeway

Create a culture of mutual respect by being adaptable in how team members carry out their jobs. Allowing individuals leeway in areas like dress code and personal space decoration might help them enjoy their job more and become more productive. Encourage your staff to modify their work process to make it more enjoyable for them. People are more inclined to take guidance and accomplish their best work when they believe someone in a leadership position cares about their well-being as a person.

## Meet Your Own Standards

Show your staff that you hold yourself to the same standards that you ask of them by setting a good example. Even though your workload is more flexible as a manager, it is crucial to demonstrate that you are a team player by keeping to the same deadlines and expectations that you set for the rest of your staff. To demonstrate you are invested in the team's success, communicate with others about the efforts you are making to complete your part in the project. Effective managers expect the same of themselves as they do their teams.

**Organize Regular Check-ins**

Hold regular group and one-on-one sessions to evaluate the development of each individual under your supervision. When high-performing employees feel overburdened, it is crucial to take the initiative as a leader to inquire about their workload and any obstacles they may have encountered. Keep a record of what you talk about at each check-in so you can discover common concerns or long-term patterns that need specific attention on an organizational or procedural level.

## MISTAKES THAT FIRST-TIME MANAGERS SHOULD AVOID

First-time managers hardly ever get training preparing them for their new role. So, as you transition into your new role, it's inevitable you'll make mistakes. However, if you're properly prepared, there are some common missteps you can avoid.

**Failing to delegate**

Your job responsibilities change when you step into a managerial position. You are now responsible for ensuring that your team completes its work and for your team members' success; you're no longer an individual contributor ticking tasks off a to-do list. You need to guard against that and instead train your team in said tasks. If you're too busy tackling tasks, you can't effectively do your job of supervising, coaching, and supporting your team.

**Getting bogged down by the details**

You need to step away from tasks as soon as you delegate them to someone else. When they have autonomy over their work, employees become happier. As a manager, keeping up with the specifics of every project is near impossible. Making sure projects are on track and tracking team members' progress is important. However, if you get involved in the details, you'll find yourself starting to micromanage. Making sure your team is working on meaningful projects that align with organizational milestones is what you should focus on instead. What is each task's contribution to the long-term goals of the team? You should not concern yourself with the details but focus your attention on the bigger picture.

**Not asking 'why'**

Sometimes new managers find themselves mimicking their predecessors instead of just being themselves. It's easy to default to the way work was done by your predecessor, but remember, you don't need to. Don't be afraid to ask "Why this approach?" when a new project comes up, and you'll know that it's time your team's approach is reevaluated if the answer to this is "Because that is how we've always done it." Is it still necessary to do this work? Is there a more efficient way to achieve the desired result? If you don't ask "Why?", you won't know.

**Changing too much in a rush**

You can ask your team about the processes that are in place, but you can't disrupt too many processes too soon. Before drastically changing how things work, take time to understand the organizational culture and your team members' goals. You'll likely find some incremental improvements you can make—such as removing an unnecessary meeting from the team's calendar or streamlining an over-complicated approval process—through your conversations with your team. Listen more than you talk, so you can truly understand what help is needed and where.

**Avoidance of tough decisions and conversation**

Approximately three hours per week is spent dealing with the workplace crisis in the United States. It's possible you won't be the exception. You need to know how to manage difficult conversations rather than avoid them. Your team's morale could get affected when you take a long time to address issues because the longer you wait, the worse it becomes. If a team member is underperforming, for example, those who pick up the slack will be negatively affected. It's never a good idea to let problems fester.

You can't avoid confrontation and difficult decisions by just saying 'yes.' You need to be strategic about your promises because the decisions you make impact your team's workload. Things normally do not end well when you try to please everyone.

**Not putting trust first**

According to research, employees are happier and make an extra effort in their work when they feel trusted by their manager (Lester & Brower, 2003). Set aside time and have a one-on-one meeting with each person on your team. Find out what their professional goals are during these check-ins. Is there a project they would like to work on or a workshop they would like to attend to gain particular skills and experience?

Practice transparency in those one-on-ones. You can build trust with your team by talking openly about the organization's goals and challenges. This can help your employees understand their roles and individual contribution to the organization's overall success.

**Not having mentors**

Informing an employee that they are under-performing or that you can't guarantee a promotion or raise is not new. Many other managers have had to do that, and so will you. It's important that you have someone you can turn to for advice when those difficult conversations arise. You can hopefully avoid a few mistakes by learning from a mentor's mistakes. Don't get discouraged when you make mistakes, because you are definitely going to make some. Your first managerial role is a learning process, and you are not expected to know everything. Own the mistakes and move on if you slip up, and ask for help where necessary.

**Speaking in the singular first person 'I'**

New managers can sometimes fall into the habit of only using 'I,' 'me,' and 'my' instead of 'we,' 'us,' and 'ours'—they fail to think in terms of the team. This is a major pitfall. You should always remember the team, even though this newfound power is a personal achievement. A shift in language, though seemingly insignificant, goes a long way in building an environment that encourages team spirit and teamwork. An effective manager will do everything that needs to be done to make sure their team members know they play a valuable role. They will also know that the success of the team translates to individual success and, as a manager, you can't have one without the other.

### Talking more than you listen

To be mindful of how you communicate is just as important as paying attention to the language you use. Your efforts can backfire if you end up talking more than you listen because you are too focused on becoming the best leader you can be. First-time managers should focus on the concerns and needs of their team members and stakeholders at every stage to avoid this. Doing so can ease the transition into your new role and help you improve communication with your team.

As you move into your first managerial role, it's inevitable that you'll make mistakes. Take these setbacks as opportunities to learn. Being perfect at your job doesn't translate to being a great manager. Being a great manager is about learning continuously and adapting to the changes in your environment so you can lead your team as best you can; it's not about being perfect at your job. Consider asking other managers for advice as you prepare to move into your first managerial position. Find out how they prepared themselves for the job, what mistakes they made and could have avoided, and what advice they would give to their past selves. Additionally, improve your managerial skills and sign up for mentorship opportunities through your workplace or look for an online course on the basics of management.

4

# DELEGATING WORK

Delegating necessitates understanding your team's capabilities and the tactics they employ to perform their tasks. You must also have a broad awareness of how many assigned activities interact to achieve a common goal. Delegating entails explicitly defining what has to be achieved, the success criteria, and the project completion deadline.

Delegating duties to those who are most suited for them improves the overall quality of your team's work. Spreading the burden of a project among numerous individuals rather than attempting to handle everything oneself helps everyone to focus on the quality of their work rather than hurrying to make a deadline.

Encourage your team members to take on greater responsibility by assigning key duties to them. This allows everyone to discover their strengths and build new abilities in the workplace. Trusting your coworkers to participate in a project fosters a team culture of empowerment and professional development. Working on your duties while also checking in with your team on the progress of delegated projects demonstrates your ability to multitask and prioritize: two critical management qualities that may help you advance your career. Delegation is a vital problem-solving method, particularly when you have a short deadline and few resources. When a team member is unable to come to work, reassigning responsibilities to other team members might help you fulfill high-priority goals or rearrange workflow.

## STRATEGIES FOR EFFECTIVE DELEGATION

Try each of these tactics when you practice delegating duties to others to make the process smoother, more productive, and more consistent.

**Learn to accept assistance**

Effective delegating entails trusting people and accepting feedback. Because they are so committed to their own achievement, many people who are normally diligent and dedicated have difficulty delegating chores to others. Learning to trust that others can fulfill your quality standards empowers you to effectively delegate. Starting with minor chores to get accustomed with the delegation process will help you create trust and become more comfortable asking for help.

**Classify priorities**

Make a clear strategy for identifying when certain jobs should be allocated. Sort projects according to the amount of work required, the abilities required, and the forthcoming deadlines. Your priority system can assist you in analyzing all that needs to be done and rapidly determining what you need to outsource to others.

## Understand when to delegate

Delegation is a crucial skill to have, but it is not the right strategy for every situation. If you are the only person with the necessary degree of competence to do a task, delegating it to others may not result in the best outcome. When you have coworkers who have the requisite time and abilities to do the assignment effectively, delegate. Make sure you are not over-burdening a team member in your attempt to assist others.

## Know your team

As mentioned earlier, know each team member's strengths, weaknesses, preferences, dislikes, and habits. One teammate may be able to do specific tasks quicker than others on your team, and knowing this ahead of time is critical for distributing responsibilities in a planned, goal-oriented manner. Giving your team work that they like to complete will help keep them engaged and invested in a project.

## Allocate decision-making power

Be explicit about what decisions your team members have the right to make, in addition to allocating particular duties to them. If an employee is confused about whether they have the power to make a decision concerning a project, it might cause the project to be delayed. Inform your team that they have the authority and obligation to manage all parts of a certain task, and that they can transfer decision-making authority when necessary.

## Be clear in your instructions

When delegating a task, offer precise instructions on when and how you want them to do it. It is possible that you may need to teach others the fundamentals of a skill before they can accomplish it on their own the first time. Make yourself available to answer clarifying inquiries and assist your staff with adjusting to new methods. While this might take time, it prevents errors and allows that teammate to complete the activity with less assistance the next time.

**Explain your thinking**

Give your staff a clear explanation of why you've assigned them a new responsibility. When you adjust someone's typical workload, let them know why you decided they were the right person for the job and how it fits within the scope of their position or career ambitions. This makes everyone feel more committed to their task and motivates them to take on new duties rather than feeling like they are doing someone else's job.

**Follow up**

Check up on the progress of allocated tasks to ensure they are being completed as planned. You are ultimately accountable for the output, even if you delegate a task to someone else. Something as basic as sending an email asking if anyone requires assistance may keep the entire project on schedule. Some people may flourish with more supervision than others, so discuss how you can best assist those who need more supervision within your team.

**Provide and solicit comments**

Evaluate how successful your team was in carrying out the tasks you set throughout the project. This will help you and the team identify possible issues before they turn into problems.

Constructive criticism is critical for professional development and displaying clear expectations. Similarly, solicit input on any difficulties that arose throughout the assignment and how you could have better assisted them. Employee feedback might help you improve how you issue instructions or adjust your management style to better support their productivity.

**Express appreciation**

Saying thank you on a frequent basis shows your employees that you appreciate them taking on the work you entrust to them. Even if taking on extra chores is part of a person's job, being grateful might make them feel appreciated and motivated to take on more responsibilities in the future.

HOW TO DELEGATE DUTIES

The following guidelines will help ensure effective delegation of duties:

**Inform your team on the project's eventual aim**

Knowing where and when they are scheduled to accomplish goals can assist your team in establishing protocols and successfully managing their time.

**Define project parameters**

This will lead to a discussion on the scope of each person's involvement in finishing the project, at which point you should explicitly outline milestones, dates, and how your team may reach out to you for assistance.

### Monitor the project's development as a group

Establishing and sharing deadlines can assist everyone to know what to aim for, but you must follow up on a frequent basis to review progress and identify any barriers that may impede the project's overall success. Maintain your emphasis on the outcomes rather than the process.

### Acknowledge a job well done

One of the most powerful motivators you can give to your team is recognition. Feeling successful and appreciated motivates them to continue growing and achieving the finest outcomes possible.

Keep the following considerations in mind when assigning tasks to your team members:

### Have a clear understanding of your team

As mentioned at the beginning of this chapter, knowing the capabilities of each team member is important for delegation purposes. When you know your team, you will be able to assign tasks properly, ensuring the successful implementation of a project.

### Project proportion

According to Pareto's Principle, one should never delegate the 20% of the work that accounts for 80% of the outcome. This implies delegating from the bottom up; lower-risk and less-sensitive activities may be assigned to someone with the necessary expertise, freeing up your time to focus on the overall project.

**The team's workloads**

Adding jobs to an already overburdened workload effectively sets your employee up for failure. Delegate fairly to guarantee that the project is completed on schedule while also keeping your personnel engaged and confident.

## TYPES OF DELEGATION

In a business, delegation may take numerous forms based on the responsibilities assigned and the amount of trust placed in those doing them. When managers trust and empower the people they delegate work to, the team members and the organization benefit. These six delegation examples will help you understand how delegation works:

**Giving detailed instructions**

The most basic type of delegation entails instructing someone exactly what to do. The individual giving the work makes all decisions in this sort of delegation, while the person executing the task just follows their directions. This form of delegation means the individual delegating spends a significant amount of time instructing and following up on every detail with the person to whom they assigned. This can be time consuming. It may, however, be an excellent technique to ensure that the person getting their new assignment fully understands how they need to perform.

**Delegation with veto power**

Another alternative is to delegate tasks while exercising veto power. Someone in this scenario requests that a coworker undertakes duties and makes choices on their behalf. They do, however, assess the work of the other person and either approve or veto it. This sort of delegation guarantees that the original authority holder keeps control. This form of delegation can assist the employee who has been allocated a new duty in learning how to delegate tasks efficiently in the future.

**Delegating research required for decision-making**

Some managers assign the research process to other staff to help them reach a decision on something. The team member performs extensive study and reports back to the manager who outsourced the assignment to them. The research is used by the person who delegated for whatever they are working on. While the individual who did the study has entire authority over this work, the person who delegated retains authority over the outcome.

**Complete delegation**

Full delegation necessitates the total transfer of duties and decision-making authority. This form of delegation demonstrates total faith in others, which may be quite empowering for those who are allocated chores. People should only utilize complete delegation if they are confident that they are delegating responsibilities to highly trained, dependable, and capable staff.

**Delegating but reserving the right to intervene**

Managers can also encourage team members to undertake certain duties while retaining the authority to intervene. This indicates that another party makes and implements choices. The person who delegated may, however, interfere and change the decision. If you delegate a task to a team member and you find yourself having to make amendments or reverse part of their decision, it is important that you explain your reasons for making those changes. This teaches them how to make better judgments about allocated work in the future.

**Delegating tasks and reporting responsibilities**

Managers can delegate jobs and request that the person allocated to the assignment report back on the project's completion. The individual who delegated hands over control and trusts the other person to do the task as they see fit. While the individual who completes the assignment reports back to the person who delegated it to them, their work is unaltered. Delegating in this manner empowers staff and shows that they are trusted.

## DOS AND DON'TS OF DELEGATING

As mentioned earlier in this chapter, delegating for the first time is a nerve wracking experience. However, how you delegate ensures whether you have control over the end product or result. For a positive delegation experience, it's important to know what you should do and what you shouldn't do when delegating.

**What you should do:**

- **Priorities should be articulated.** What is the goal of the delegation? Is it to train the team member to take over the project, or is it to free up your time? What is the deadline for the submission of the project? Making sure your employee understands your priorities will help them make decisions regarding time commitments on other projects, communication, and so forth.
- **Have guidelines in place.** Make sure the employee knows how much time you've allocated for the

completion of a task. You don't want to find yourself in a situation where an employee has spent hours on something you expected to be a 30-minute task. Also inform the employee what the communication lines are on the particular task. To avoid misunderstandings, communicate clearly from the onset.

- **Be supportive.** Do not use the sink-or-swim approach; rather, empower your team members to succeed. Provide all the necessary information, including examples of comparable work. Make it easy for them to ask questions and, at certain points of the project, check in to see how they are progressing.
- **Employees should feel comfortable disagreeing with you.** It may be a bad experience for a team member if they take on responsibilities they feel they are not ready for, even if you think they are ready for greater responsibility. Do not force matters; it's not worth the anxiety it will cause. Find another employee to take on the task.
- **After completion, have a conversation about the experience.** Find out how things went and ascertain whether there are things you could have done differently to improve the experience. Use the meeting to gently guide them if they made mistakes during the project. It's important that you praise them for their output and thank them for the work they've accomplished. Lastly, find out if they would be comfortable and willing to do the task again.

**What you shouldn't do:**

- **Start micromanaging.** You need to provide your employee with enough space to learn on their own, even if this exercise is for training purposes. An employee's confidence in their abilities will be undermined if they get the impression that you don't trust them. Take your hands off the reins and keep them off, as this will indicate your trust and belief in them.
- **Underestimate the project deadline.** Be cautious about underestimating the length of time it will take for the project to be complete. Your employee may need to do a number of things to help get the project going, even though implementation may take you a week. Also take into account that your team members may require you to take the time to provide guidance if they encounter some unexpected roadblocks. Things don't always go as smoothly as we would like them to, so always provide a buffer by giving extra time.
- **Delegate tasks that require you specifically.** Be selective. Some tasks should not be delegated because they may require your insight or expertise. The important tasks should remain in your to-do list and not be delegated.
- **Delegate projects that you don't want to do.** Don't be the type of manager who avoids doing unpleasant tasks by delegating them. Your employees will know it and they will not appreciate that. A willingness to do the menial, unappealing, and aggravating tasks for the good of the organization is what good leadership means. Bad management is passing off tasks because you don't like them, and it's a sure way of losing the respect of your employees.

## 5

## GOAL-SETTING

One of a manager's most important responsibilities is effectively setting and using goals to manage performance, which is critical for achieving organizational objectives and helping team members develop their skills and capabilities.

Without goals, team members might get disoriented, unsure of what to accomplish or whether what they are doing is proper and essential. Teams who have defined goals tend to experience tremendous improvements, often even double what they would have achieved without goals.

As a manager, you will get many opportunities to contribute to the organization's overarching goals and objectives. After years of living with numerous challenges as a regular employee—and maybe complaining about them—you finally have the opportunity to make meaningful contributions toward improving them. Use your new, stronger voice to impact long-term strategy by using your awareness of your local operation's strengths and constraints. The purpose and vision of the organization will lead to goals. In most circumstances, this will incorporate high-level financial and other resources, as well as customer objectives. As a low-level manager, you must translate these bigger aims into organizational goals for your particular department or team.

For example, suppose the organization sets a profit margin target. In order to produce the intended profit, the sales department must meet a particular revenue objective and the operations department must meet a given cost of goods sold.

When setting departmental goals, it's best to involve team members. Employees will be more creative in determining what needs to happen locally and more invested in reaching those final goals if they fully grasp the overarching purpose, vision, strategy, and top-level goals. Setting departmental objectives requires you, as the manager, to establish the 'how' of achieving the goals at a local level. This cannot be just accepting a top-down objective assignment. It should instead be a collaborative articulation of an objective based on existing and planned functional capacity. If there is a considerable difference between present performance and the objective, yearning for better results will not achieve them.

## THE BENEFITS OF SETTING GOALS

Any team and organization needs to have goals to succeed. Goals provide leaders and employees with guidance and direction, as well an understanding of the performance of each individual on the team. Over and above that, there are many other reasons goal-setting is such an important practice.

Let's go through some of the benefits.

- **Goals promote team alignment.** Employees get confused about how their work impacts the success of the organization if they lack information or don't have an understanding of organizational goals. Without clear goals, there'll be an overlap of work; employees will

interfere in one another's work and be confused about their responsibilities.
- **Goals provide clarity.** Research indicates that there is a 20–25% improvement in the performance of teams with clear goals (van der Hoek et al., 2016). The reason for this is employees become more productive when their efforts are focused in the right direction. By setting goals, you give your team a structure and a clear plan of action as a team, and as individuals.
- **Goals help you prioritize work.** Once the goals have been established, they may be tackled in the order of their importance. This enables jobs to be done on schedule and in the correct order. The capacity to prioritize goals demonstrates an employee's ability to plan ahead and focus. This better prepares them and clarifies what work has to be performed and by when.

For goals to work, they need to be simple, measurable, attainable, relevant, and time-bound—anything less gives no direction at all and is, therefore, meaningless. You may have heard of SMART objectives in the context of goal planning. So, let's take a closer look at this.

## WHAT ARE SMART GOALS?

SMART stands for **specific, measurable, attainable, relevant,** and **time-bound**. Each component of the SMART framework contributes to the creation of a goal that is well-planned, explicit, and trackable.

You may have previously established objectives that were difficult to fulfill because they were too broad, too aggressive, or poorly defined. Working for an ill-defined objective might feel difficult and unattainable. Creating SMART objectives can assist in resolving these issues. Whether you're creating personal or professional objectives, the SMART goal framework may provide a solid basis for success.

Below is a demonstration of how to transform a goal like "I want to be in leadership" into a SMART goal. Your objectives are described by the words in bold.

- **S stands for Specific**

Be as explicit and specific as possible about your goals. The more specific your objective, the better you'll figure out how to reach it.

Example: "I'd want to **manage a development team for a fledgling software firm**."

- **M stands for Measurable**

What evidence will demonstrate that you are making progress toward your goal? For example, if you want to lead a development team for a new software firm, you may track your success by the number of management roles you've applied for or interviews you've had.

Setting milestones along the route will allow you to re-evaluate and pivot where necessary. Remember to reward yourself in tiny but meaningful ways as you reach your milestones.

Example: "I'll apply to **three** available roles as the manager of a development team at a tech firm."

- **A stands for Attainable**

Is your goal realistic and attainable? Setting objectives that you can practically achieve within a specific time frame can help you stay motivated and focused. Using the previous example of obtaining a job directing a development team, you should be aware of the qualifications, experience, and abilities required for that role. Before you begin working toward a goal, consider if it is something you can do right away or whether there are more preparatory measures you need to take to be ready.

Example: "**I will update my CV with necessary qualifications** so that I may apply to three available positions for the manager of a development team at a tech organization."

- R stands for Relative

Consider whether the goals you establish for yourself are relevant. Each of your objectives should be consistent with your values and broader, long-term objectives. If a goal does not add to your overall aims, you should reconsider it. Consider why the goal is important to you, how reaching it will benefit you, and how it will contribute to your long-term objectives.

Example: "**To reach my objective of becoming a leader**, I will update my CV with necessary skills and apply to three available positions for the manager of a development team at a tech organization."

- T stands for Time-bound

What is your desired time frame? An end date might assist you, motivate you, and help you prioritize. For example, if you want to advance to a more senior job, you may allow yourself six months. If you haven't attained your objective by then, think about why. Your deadline may have been unreasonable, you may have encountered unanticipated hurdles, or your objective may have been unattainable.

Example: "To reach my objective of being in leadership, I will update my CV with necessary skills **this week** so that I may apply to three available positions for the manager of a development team at a tech organization."

The SMART goal framework describes the actions you'll need to take, the resources you'll need to get there, and milestones that signal progress along the route. You are more likely to attain your objective efficiently and effectively if you use SMART goals.

## GOAL-SETTING MISTAKES

Sometimes organizations and managers make mistakes when setting goals. Here, we discuss the most common ones.

- **Exclude employees in the process.** Excluding employees from the goal setting process is a mistake managers often make. Employees should participate in goal-setting in collaboration with the manager. Involving employees in goal-setting makes them more accountable. Productivity and job satisfaction increase when employees don't feel the goals were imposed on them.
- **Goals that are not aligned.** When the goals are not aligned, employees struggle to understand their role in the bigger picture. Effective employee goals are aligned with the team, as well as departmental and organizational goals. Employees become more engaged and productive at work when they understand their role in the success of the organization.
- **Inflexible goals.** The objective of a goal can change even while an employee is working toward it. It's important to set goals that are easy to update. Employees are negatively affected by static goals. Most managers make the mistake of waiting for performance reviews before updating or revisiting goals.

- **Not tracking progress.** Failure to revisit goals also implies that the goals are not tracked, and this results in employees not knowing whether what they're doing is right or wrong. With the help of you, as the manager, employees should identify their key milestones with timelines to achieve them. From time to time, review the employee's progress and share feedback with them. Doing this will help team members stay aligned with organizational goals and focused on achieving their own goals.
- **Failing to recognize and reward employees.** You should take time to acknowledge and reward your team members; this is as crucial as setting goals. Employees become motivated to achieve more when you reward and recognize them for small wins. They will get derailed from their goals and feel undervalued and unimported if you don't recognize them for their efforts.

# 6

# DIVERSITY AND INCLUSION

Workplace diversity is essential for growing a successful business. For starters, workplace diversity means that individuals can bring something unique to the table. This can be cultural awareness or viewing things from a different perspective. As a result, a diverse team can be a source of inspiration, innovation, and success.

Managing a diverse workforce enables you to encourage creativity and innovation. Your older employees have a long-term perspective, whereas your younger employees are technologically savvy. Consider what solutions they can provide to make your business more convenient and future-proof. There's a set of skills that new managers can learn to help create safe environments in which diverse teams can thrive. There is no single way to prepare yourself or your team for success, particularly in the area of diversity management, so we've provided several options to get started.

## CHALLENGES OF LEADING DIVERSE TEAMS

Managing a diverse group of people can be difficult for a variety of reasons that may not become apparent until you are in that position of leadership.

- **Lack of experience:** You are suddenly responsible for a wide range of people with diverse backgrounds and experiences, including some you don't have, can't see, and didn't even know existed.
- **Barriers to communication:** Managing a diverse team may imply that certain individuals speak a foreign language. This might lead to a communication breakdown among staff, potentially impacting production. Hiring multilingual employees to undertake translations might help you prevent this. You may also select from a variety of translation applications on the market. Consider sending personnel to language schools to learn new languages. As an added benefit, this will help them communicate with overseas consumers.

Bridging the communication gap among employees will help your firm expand and create new opportunities for success.

- **Intersectionality:** When you look at your team, you may notice or be given visible and disclosed indicators of diversity. Consider gender, race, and age. However, diversity can also refer to a broader set of characteristics that a group or individual possesses. This includes a variety of cultures, sexual orientations, socioeconomic status, physical abilities, political affiliations, and religions.

- **Different views on professional etiquette:** Traditions vary according to culture. Furthermore, they have distinct ideals and manners in the workplace. This may lead to misconceptions among team members, and perhaps conflict. In Japanese culture, for example, it is traditional to wait until the host requests for you to sit before entering someone else's office. As a result, a Japanese employee may find it disrespectful when a colleague from the United States enters their office and instantly takes a seat. To combat this and avoid workplace conflict, ensure that your staff understand and respect each other's customs.
- **Biases from our backgrounds:** Even when our self-awareness allows us to identify some gaps in diversity, our biases can prevent us from seeing others. As a manager who strongly identifies with and considers their gender and race, for example, you can determine whether or not your team is inclusive of people of different races and genders. However, you may not be as quick to consider an imbalance in other diversity markers such as physical ability or political affiliation.

WHAT MAKES A LEADER INCLUSIVE?

There are a number of behaviors and traits that distinguish inclusive managers. In this book, we'll cover only some of them.

- **Authentic commitment:** Inclusive managers demonstrate genuine dedication to diversity by questioning the current quo, holding others responsible, and making diversity and inclusion a personal priority.

- **Bias awareness:** They are conscious of personal blind spots as well as system weaknesses and strive hard to maintain meritocracy.
- **They are humble:** They do not shine a light on themselves and are modest about their abilities and accomplishments. Their humility makes them focus on others and not on their own abilities and talents. They are not afraid to own their mistakes, and they make room for others to participate and contribute.
- **Genuine interest in others:** They have an open mind and a profound curiosity about others, listen without judgment, and attempt to understand people around them with empathy.
- **True collaborators:** They empower others, pay attention to a variety of thought and psychological safety, and prioritize team cohesiveness.
- **Empathetic:** Inclusive leaders have an appreciation for what others might be experiencing. They embrace compassion and encourage interaction in order to encourage meaningful connections with others.
- **Sensitive to cultural differences:** They are aware of the cultures of others and adapt as needed.
- **Build relationships:** Inclusive leaders spend time getting to know what matters to their team members, other employees, and their peers. For inclusive leaders, building relationships is about understanding and appreciating a person in their entirety.

## COMPETENCIES TO IMPROVE WHEN MANAGING DIVERSE TEAMS

As a manager, you not only need to be aware of diversity gaps, but also to recalibrate how you move through your workplace. This entails becoming an intuitive, supportive, and aware leader, which can help you in cultivating a diverse team that performs optimally and thrives.

However, for a diverse team to thrive, it needs effective management and leadership. There are a number of formal systems and soft skills you can focus on honing to get started in this area.

*Formal Systems*

## Feedback channels

Feedback channels are essential in any team, especially one with a diverse set of opinions.

Formal feedback channels between managers and team members hold everyone accountable for speaking up. They enable every voice to be officially heard and every opinion to be valued. They also provide you, the manager, with information about issues your team members are facing or flaws you can correct.

Whether you use digital surveys or one-on-one meetings, you're allowing different points of view to be expressed on a diverse team. In an environment where your team's or direct reports' identities differ from yours, you may miss or misinterpret something that causes a problem for others. Prepare your team and yourself to provide constructive, safe feedback.

## Conflict resolution skills

Conflict resolution may conjure up some frightening images. A manager who acts as a third wheel in a feud between two irate employees. Or a manager caught between two opposing groups, bottlenecking a project and lowering employee morale.

Instead, consider conflict resolution as a positive exercise that can help your team's diversity to be a catalyst for growth. Different needs, values, customs, and violations of personal boundaries are some of the most common causes of conflict in teams with diverse members. Miscommunication is at the root of many of these types of conflicts.

Consider training in conflict resolution for yourself and your entire team. This relieves you of the burden of being the only person capable of handling difficult situations. However, it will also enable individuals to eventually identify and address their own diversity, equity, and inclusion issues.

Additional opportunities for learning and development could include:

- **Unconscious bias:** Training to assist teams in understanding and identifying how unconscious biases enter the workplace.
- **Perspective-taking:** Exercises to help employees develop empathy and comprehend a colleague's point of view.
- **Cross-cultural trainers:** Coaching and training centered on how cultural differences affect teams.

*Soft Skills*

**Self-awareness and emotional intelligence**

Not all managers enter their positions with a critical level of awareness about how their identity affects them as leaders. We are all influenced by societal pressures and norms throughout our lives, which can result in unconscious but unmistakable biases. The stereotypes, media, and personal experiences in typical workplaces can all have an impact on us.

For example:

- Male managers promote and compensate men differently than women in comparable positions.
- People design workplaces that do not take a variety of physical abilities into account.
- People from a specific social group consistently hire those who reflect their own interests and community.
- Those in Human Resources in charge of holiday closures may fail to recognize holidays that are not part of their own religious practice.

We bring habits and prejudices into the office whether we like it or not. However, practicing self-awareness will help you identify what habits, biases, and harmful behaviors you exhibit with your colleagues.

Consider getting to know yourself better to develop your emotional intelligence. Ask yourself the following questions to discover how your personal identity may be influencing how your employees interpret your actions.

What effect might your socioeconomic status, gender, or race have on:

- how you make hiring decisions?
- how you communicate with different people?
- how you delegate tasks in the office?
- how your organization handles social events or celebrations?

**Effective communication skills**

Good communication skills can be applied to teams in a variety of ways. This includes how you communicate with individuals, the group as a whole, and how you encourage those individuals to communicate with one another.

Creating environments that encourage open communication across the board, as a manager, demonstrates that you value diverse voices and opinions.

Use and demonstrate good communication skills by:

- Comfortably discussing difficult topics and situations to demonstrate to your team that you are willing to be vulnerable.
- Managing conflicts by encouraging both parties to communicate with each other with respect and rationally.

**Empathy**

Empathizing with your team's experiences will not only help you respond to conflicts more effectively. It can also assist you in proactively shaping environments in which diverse team members perform better and thrive.

When your employees express concerns, truly listening to them can help you understand what they are going through. You can then use your insights to create an environment that allows everyone to excel.

For example: You might notice a change in a team member's demeanor at work. You know they've gotten a big new project, but you assumed they'd be excited. Instead of jumping to conclusions, invite them to talk about what they're actually feeling.

In a brief conversation, you might hear them say they're feeling overwhelmed and interpret it as poor time management. However, if you empathize and ask the right questions, you may learn that they are missing time with their families to be at work because systems to help them be efficient are not in place.

## OVERCOMING CHALLENGES OF WORKPLACE DIVERSITY

There are many things a manager can do to help overcome the challenges associated with diversity in the workplace.

**More underrepresented minorities should be recruited**

While this may appear to be an obvious point, unconscious prejudice and other factors might limit the number of minority candidates who make it through the recruiting process. Consider incorporating "blind hiring" approaches into your employment procedure for your team. Blind hiring is any strategy that makes the recruiting process anonymous. This might involve eliminating identifying demographic information from resumes, having candidates participate in anonymous pre-hire testing, or even conducting a blind interview by chat bot or questionnaire.

**Utilize diversity education and mentorship**

Over the last few years, many of the most successful Fortune 500 companies have introduced diversity training. Although it appears to be a remedy, investigations on its effectiveness have been inconsistent. If your company wants to see meaningful change in terms of diversity and inclusion, make sure that at least one of each employee's objectives is to promote diversity and inclusion. Completing a project with a diverse team, mentoring someone from a different background, or participating in team-building activities might be examples of this.

**Facilitate various communication methods**

Everyone in a diverse team will not communicate in the same

manner. It is critical for the success of your team that everyone's voice be heard. Begin by establishing a communication-friendly environment. Lead by example and demonstrate to people in your company that they do not need to be frightened to speak out or express views and ideas at work, regardless of the cultural norms they are accustomed to. Allow individuals to interact efficiently using whichever manner they like, whether by email, in person, or through a collaborative tool. Consider using an anonymous communication mechanism for more sensitive topics, and make sure individuals realize there will be no consequences for reporting legitimate issues.

## THE BENEFITS OF A DIVERSE WORKFORCE

When you put a diverse group of people in the same room, you'll receive a diversity of viewpoints and thoughts that can help your business. This will help your company to expand in a variety of ways.

The following are six benefits of a diverse staff for your company:

### 1. Improved creativity and ideas

When a group of like-minded people gather together, they will come up with similar ideas. This is because their thought patterns are quite similar. However, by mixing various individuals together, you may create a workforce that is more prone to creativity and invention—two essential factors for success.

A diverse staff will be able to share distinct viewpoints and generate new ideas. A notable example is the Disney brand, which is a diverse organization with over 200,000 people globally.

## 2. Revenue growth

Increasing income is a top concern for any business. You will get closer to your ultimate aim of raising earnings by reaping the benefits of a diverse workforce. According to recent Boston Consulting Group research, businesses with a diverse staff and enhanced creativity made 19% more revenue than businesses with lower diversity ratings (Lorenzo, 2020). The evidence is in the numbers.

## 3. A bigger talent pool

When workforce diversification is part of your organizational values and you commit to it, you attract a larger talent pool with applicants you may not previously have considered. A diverse workforce brings with it fresh ideas and provides new abilities to your organization.

## 4. Enhanced productivity

Diversity and productivity are inextricably linked. According to research by McKinsey & Company, diversifying your staff may increase efficiency by 35% (Hunt et al., 2015). A varied team is more likely to comprehend your clients' wants and devise solutions to meet them. Diversity in the workplace will boost employee morale and create a drive to be more successful and efficient at work. This will significantly boost your organization's productivity.

## 5. Connect to a broader range of customers

A varied staff is required if you want to reach a wide spectrum of consumers. By recruiting people from various backgrounds, languages, and so on, you may ensure that your firm appeals to a broader target market. Your staff will be able to interact with customers from various walks of life, since they come from diverse backgrounds.

**6. Decrease in employee turnover**

Employees will feel appreciated and welcomed in a workplace that promotes diversity and inclusion. This will guarantee that your employees are content. Happy employees will stay with your firm longer, which means you'll spend less money and effort recruiting. You'll have more time and money to invest in your firm if you reduce staff turnover.

Creating a diverse organizational culture provides you with a distinct edge in the industry by allowing you to build goods that appeal to a diverse population; an advantage that you might not get in a homogenous corporate culture. Diverse input improves brainstorming, creativity, idea development, and innovation. If everyone in the room exclusively likes gray and white, all of your items will mirror that theme. Product development and innovation benefit from diversity. Finally, the value of a varied workplace is not just doing the right thing, but also providing a new point of view.

For many of the world's largest and most successful organizations and corporations, diversity and inclusion has become a business imperative. Here's a list of a few of them and a summary of how they've diversified their workforces successfully:

- **Sodexo:** Sodexo, is a food services and facilities company, explicitly included age, gender, and sexual orientation in their diverse hiring strategy, emphasizing gender equality. Sodexo has made gender equality a priority in its whole business strategy for the past 20 years, and it has paid off: Sodexo was nominated to the 2020 Bloomberg Gender Equality Index, which assesses

the financial success of enterprises committed to gender equality.
- **Johnson & Johnson (J&J):** Johnson & Johnson, a multinational medical device, pharmaceutical, and consumer goods company, has a diversity-and-inclusion strategy that aims to "maximize the worldwide potential of diversity and inclusion to generate improved business results and long-term competitive advantage." J&J does this through employee resource groups, mentorship programs, and the incorporation of diversity and inclusion efforts into day-to-day operations.
- **Mastercard:** Mastercard has been ranked in the top 10 for diversity by DiversityInc for four years in a row as a result of its commitment to several programs. For example, Mastercard is dedicated to fair pay for equal labor, uses technology for social good, and sponsors Girls4Tech, a STEM curriculum that provides mentorship and career guidance to girls aged 8–12. Mastercard also offers practical, direct employee benefits like coverage for sex reassignment surgery, coverage for same-sex domestic partners, and assistance with fertility treatment, surrogacy, and adoption.

7

# PURPOSE

Nobody wants to feel like just a cog in the machine. People want to feel there's meaning in the work they do and to see the impact it has on others. They become more engaged, innovative, and productive as a result. That is not a surprise or a revelation. It's just common sense. People who live their purpose at work outperform those who do not. They are also more healthy, resilient, and likely to stay with the company. Furthermore, when employees believe that their purpose is aligned with that of the organization, the benefits include increased loyalty, employee engagement, and people become more inclined to recommend the organization—as an employer, potential business partner, and client—to others. According to research carried out by McKenzie & Company on two-thirds of U.S.-based employees, 70% of employees surveyed said that work defines their sense of purpose (Dhingra et al., 2021). As a manager, you, therefore, have an important role to play in ensuring that your team members find a purpose they can believe in and live by.

## LEADERSHIP AND PURPOSE

Today, our idea of leadership is undergoing significant transformations. Leadership is no longer defined by a few individuals at the top dictating how an organization should be operated. Leadership is now diffused across an organization's many levels. Mission-driven leadership is a leadership style that prioritizes an organization's purpose or values over development and profit. A purpose-driven organization approaches its goal and vision with a deliberate values-based approach. Purpose-driven leadership is a new approach that acknowledges a leader's position as an adjudicator and champion for an organization's purpose.

To lead in this way, you must uncover your leadership purpose, assist those you lead in discovering their purpose, and link people's personal purposes with that of the organization. Here are three reasons why this strategy is critical for professional success.

**Purpose holds an organization together**

According to leadership experts, purpose is critical to successfully navigating the complicated, turbulent, and ambiguous corporate environment that characterizes our current business climate. A purpose-driven leader can unite people around a single goal, which is the achievement of organizational goals. This leadership style explains to people why they do what they do. Meaning and purpose in one's job have the potential to be a powerful motivator for achieving the desired objectives. Leading with purpose at the heart is a realistic strategy to alter an organization's fabric. It converts employees into partners in the company's mission, who recognize the importance of their daily contributions to the organization's success.

## Purpose leads to higher profits

The unmistakable proof of a company plan is its impact on the bottom line. According to studies on purpose-driven leadership, meaningful businesses are more lucrative. Profit alone is no longer a sufficient motivation for employee engagement and performance. Customers and clients are also more inclined to stay involved with businesses that have a purpose. Organizations that have purpose embedded in their culture outperform those that are just concerned with profit. Profits and long-term success may be discovered through recognizing and valuing an organization's mission, regardless of market ups and downs. This demonstrates the strength of the commercial case for purpose-driven leadership techniques, which are required for long-term success.

## Employees are drawn to and engaged by a sense of purpose

A purpose-driven leader may inspire outstanding performance in themselves and those they lead, all while creating higher well-being inside the organization. According to research, 70% of millennials appreciate having a sense of purpose in their employment (Deloitte, 2018). Millennials are quickly becoming the most numerous generation in the global labor market. Providing a feeling of purpose in the workplace might thereby attract top talent. In the workplace, an emphasis on the connection of personal and organizational purpose enhances employee engagement. The organization's purpose should be communicated to employees and used as a guidepost for everything you do. Netflix's culture deck, for example, was critical to preserving their culture as they grew in their early years. They eventually made it public, and it has been viewed over 15 million times on LinkedIn alone.

What does it mean to lead with purpose? It means the following:

- **Defining reality:** Defining reality requires the leader to deliver the harsh facts to the personnel so that they understand the company's strengths and limitations in no uncertain terms. If a new industry competitor, for example, pops up in the same area and the employees start feeling worried and deflated, a leader who leads with purpose will play open cards with the employees and define reality. The leader will lay out the aspects of the organization that will place them in good standing and the areas they will have to improve to stay ahead of the competitor and retain their clients.
- **Explaining issues to the employees in a simple yet detailed manner:** A leader with a purpose is one who has a clear understanding of what the organization symbolizes and knows everything about the organization, and so has no qualms about regularly reminding people of what they need to accomplish, especially when the employees are puzzled about something. It is critical for a leader to be able to break things down into simple, uncomplicated language and relay information to employees so that they do not make mistakes while carrying out activities delegated to them by higher authorities. Such errors are a massive waste of money and time.
- **Allowing them to be part of your dream and vision as co-creators:** A person that leads with purpose knows the importance of communication with vision and plans to the employees. This leader is a visionary and shares the organization's plans because they want to inspire and encourage the employees to dream big, too. If you keep people in the dark about what you're doing and

what the organization is up to, they'll never be able to feel like they are valued and critical to the success of the organization. A leader with a purpose is someone who can bring everyone in the organization together so that everyone works together and no one is chasing their own selfish purposes or agendas.

- **Letting the employees know and understand how the work that they do is key to the organization's success:** When you lead with purpose, you make communicating to workers how their specific role influences the overall performance of the organization a priority. Leading with purpose entails not just having a feeling of purpose yourself, but also inspiring others to do the same. If people feel valued and needed, they are more likely to offer their all. Over and above making them feel important, they will also realize that having an open and transparent system means everyone needs to play their part and execute their individual responsibilities correctly. In a transparent way, when blunders or problems happen, they can be easily traced back to the source, so everyone needs to do their part.
- **Consistent and unwavering attention on the tasks and goals at hand:** When someone leads with purpose, they are exceedingly goal-oriented and they have a specific aim in mind. He will do all in his power not to stray from the road. This trait guarantees that things stay on track and that no time is wasted. It is a great trait to have as a leader. Time is extremely valuable in business, and only those who lack foresight would squander it. Meeting deadlines and focusing on the job at hand at all times is the only way to ensure that the business thrives and succeeds, regardless of how

challenging the conditions are or what hurdles may occur.

- **Implies trusting yourself and not constantly seeking others' validation:** The basic foundation of every business is its purpose. Without purpose, an organization has no anchor and can easily be derailed and go astray. Purposeful leaders understand and have a clear vision of what they want and do not make a habit of continuously seeking approval from other people. Having said that, it is crucial to highlight that a purposeful leader will seek counsel from others and make educated judgments, but at no point will they second-guess or question their decisions. This is one of the most important characteristics of a leader who leads with purpose. It is this single-mindedness of purpose that steers the organization on.

- **Understanding what needs to be done and when to do it:** A leader with purpose is someone whose sense of purpose emanates from a high level of practical insight, as well as a high level of technical competence and knowledge. Such a person is quick to think on their feet and can readily read and assess situations. For these reasons, a person who leads with purpose understands both what to do and when to do it. They have an innate capacity to make decisions that they know would greatly benefit the organization. A leader who lacks a sense of purpose is not a good leader.

Simple methods for leading your team with purpose:

- **Have a clear and specific plan of action:** You must be completely aware of what you are doing in order to lead with purpose. If you have self-doubt and are unsure of yourself or what is required of someone in your position, you'll never be able to perform what is expected of you; instead, you'll be a wanderer who acts sporadically. Having a basic plan or blueprint to work from will always assist you along the road, but if you think of any improvements that can be made to your plan along the way, you will never hesitate to make the changes.
- **Be confident no matter what:** How can a person lead with purpose if they don't believe in themselves or what they're attempting to communicate to their employees? One of the simplest methods to help you lead with purpose is to have bravery in your own convictions. Only those with confidence and the courage to dream will be able to make it big in life and lead their organizations to greater heights. Confidence and self-assurance, on the other hand, do the most, but overconfidence will not get a person very far if they have unrealistic goals with nothing backing them up .
- **Outside of work, cultivate a sense of purpose:** When organizations go all-in on instilling a sense of purpose at work, they often want to hammer it into their employees' heads. They also have a tendency to forget that outside of work, their employees have lives and purposes. Organizations should encourage and provide time and resources for their employees to pursue their interests outside of work.

A project management software company called Basecamp, for

example, offers its employees a $1,000 annual allowance to continue education. You can also offer flexible schedules to allow your employees to pursue hobbies outside of work.

- **Make work count:** Managers and leaders must recognize the importance of a team's sense of purpose. Employees today want not just an important title and a good salary. They want to know how they can help the company achieve its goals. To keep employees motivated, profit and purpose must coexist.
- **Find out what the employees' source of purpose is:** Short-term goals can be very effective in motivating employees to meet a deadline, but what about long-term motivation? People who see their jobs as a calling are more satisfied than those who see it as just a job. Researcher Amy Wrzesniewski spoke with hospital janitors who believed their role extended beyond cleaning to assisting patients in healing.

Inquiring about employees' sense of purpose can reveal surprising reasons for their motivation in their role. You can collect employee feedback and use the results to:

- improve their understanding of their responsibilities
- change responsibilities to better reflect their sense of mission
- ascertain that they are engaged in their work
- **Create opportunities for further learning and development:** Investing in the education and training of employees is one way to make them feel important, and this is true for all employees. Offering opportunities for advancement to a select few can make others feel undervalued.

Investing in an on-going learning culture will:

- increase employee confidence in their abilities
- encourage employees to take on difficult tasks

In addition to one-on-one support, you can employ communication software to help foster a learning culture. Development and learning do not always have to take the form of a standard course or manual. In an era of technology, a method such as gamification is an effective and enjoyable way of engaging employees.

- **Make collaboration an uncomplicated process:** Collaboration emphasizes the importance of the team having a common goal. If a team collaborates on a project without a clear understanding of why they're doing it, the project is bound to fail.

This is especially important in a post-pandemic world where so many employees work remotely. Spontaneous collaborations are often not possible for remote workers; they use the communication tools at their disposal to connect with colleagues and find mentors. Remote workers' ability to collaborate effectively is heavily reliant on the tools they use.

The following must be kept in mind when deciding on collaboration software:

- how it will be used
- the frequency of use on a daily basis
- how simple it is to set up the app
- security and integration capabilities of the app
- **Have a recognition and reward program:** It's all too easy to get caught up in the daily grind. As a result, recognizing and acknowledging the work and

contribution of employees to the organization and team helps them appreciate and understand why their work is important. We are inspired by how our work benefits those around us. We get a stronger sense of purpose from knowing that what we do every day makes a difference to our communities, country, and the world.

Not only major accomplishments should be recognized. Small-scale achievements are also important. However, it can be difficult to keep track of those in a large corporation. When your team is dispersed, it is not always possible to celebrate in person.

- **Include frontline employees:** The majority of advice on motivating employees is based on the assumption that all employees work in an office. But what about the ones who are not office-bound—the frontline workers?

Without the right strategy, it can be difficult giving frontline workers a sense of purpose and motivation. The lack of proper tools to motivate them makes frontline workers feel cut off from the organization for which they work.

- **Safety should be a top-of-list priority:** When they believe their employer takes their safety seriously, employees are much more likely to be invested in their work. Improving safety begins with the proper communication tools.
- **Create multiple feedback platforms:** If employees believe their feedback is welcome and treated with urgency, they will feel a sense of purpose in the workplace. Employees who believe their voices are heard are 4.6 times more likely to feel empowered to do their best work.

A survey planning checklist can help you ensure that you:

- pose questions with specific goals in mind
- use the proper tools to conduct regular surveys
- use the appropriate surveys to reach and communicate with employees

Frequent surveys demonstrate to employees that their input is valued. They can also provide you with accurate data on employee satisfaction and engagement.

- **Engage your organization's cheerleaders**: Cheerleaders are present in every organization. They are the ones who:
- are natural leaders within their teams
- speak up the most in meetings, frequently to express what others are thinking
- plan non-work events for their coworkers
- are most likely to be the 'face' of the organization

Looking at a cheerleader we know can rekindle our motivation when we've lost our sense of purpose at work. If they're enthusiastic about their work, perhaps we can be as well. However, cheerleaders' reach is limited to their immediate coworkers. By giving them a platform on a company-wide communication tool, you will be able to get employees who are not motivated to follow their lead.

- **Organizational values should be relevant**: Finally, it is worth asking the obvious question:
- Are the organization's values that were established years ago still relevant today?

We live in a world where the definition of work is evolving by the month as a result of the COVID pandemic. The face of work has changed:

- The new normal is remote work.
- Work-life balance is no longer what it once was.
- New priorities include safety and mental health awareness.

Many times, corporate values do not need to be amended because they are abstract enough to withstand change. Priorities, however, shift. Perhaps flexible scheduling and the ability to work your own hours transition from a perk to an important part of workplace offering. Perhaps improving employee access to mental health resources will also become an essential offering.

Values provide a sense of purpose to an organization and its employees. Check to see whether those values are still relevant.

Some of the most successful brands and organizations in the world are purpose-driven.

- **Tesla:** Tesla has been noted from its start for its environmental and renewable energy projects, most notably in the brand's automotive range. Tesla's mission statement is to expedite the transition to sustainable energy, but with Elon Musk at the helm, the company's ambition is to transform the world. Tesla, true to its purpose-driven goal, was fast to respond during the epidemic. During the height of the COVID epidemic, it opened its manufacturing facilities and repurposed its vehicle parts to produce ventilators for hospitals. Musk may like scandals, and is frequently forced into the spotlight as a result of them, but his competence in leading innovation and delivering on the company's promises is not to be underestimated.

This is also what distinguishes Tesla from other electric car manufacturing businesses.

- **The Cheeky Panda:** The Cheeky Panda is an eco-friendly brand that counts its success in terms of tons of carbon balanced and trees saved. Bamboo, the world's fastest-growing plant, is used to make sustainable toilet paper, kitchen tissues and rolls, and baby wipes.

When the founders visited Southeast Asia, they saw how much bamboo was tossed. When they returned, they looked into bamboo-based products. As a result, a more environmentally friendly alternative to pulp products was developed. Boots, Watsons, Amazon, and Carrefour distribute the company's products in the United States, China, Europe, and the Middle East. Its environmental impact indicates its commitment to long-term sustainability.

- **Patagonia:** Patagonia has been dubbed a model of brand purpose. This started with its founder, Yvon Chouinard, a former rock climber who is still Patagonia's principal visionary. In 2002, he vowed to give 1% of its sales revenue or 10% of its profits—whichever is greater—to grassroots environmental groups each year.

Patagonia's mission statement is reflected in every aspect of the brand. From its basic beliefs to its repair and recycling efforts and use of only organic suppliers, the company is committed to sustainability. The recycling initiative urges consumers to buy less. The corporation is also making an attempt to improve labor conditions by implementing regulations for its supplier chain and manufacturing. The firm believes in brand activism. Patagonia is committed to taking a position and upholding strong moral standards.

- **Lego:** Generations of children and adults have embraced Lego for its fun and inventive traits, but the company's shift to a focus on purpose and sustainability has truly distinguished Lego as one of the world's most significant brands.

Lego refocused their core mission and values to run environmentally responsible operations and make sustainable products in line with a higher purpose "to inspire and develop the builders of tomorrow." Lego even went so far as to end a 50-year brand partnership with Shell because Lego's environmental values no longer resonated with Shell's.

Lego is committing $400 million to support its environmental and social responsibility activities, which is a significant step toward realizing their mission. One of these goals is to use recycled or renewable materials in all Lego packaging. They are also committed to using sustainable materials in all of their primary goods.

- **Starbucks:** Starbucks rounds out the list. Due to its huge income source, the coffee giant may not appear to be an obvious pick, but the corporation has a purpose profoundly woven into their business operations, from recruiting to sourcing and supply, and into the community in which they serve.

Among the commendable practices is ensuring that its partners or baristas are put through education and training programs that prepare them to be able to take up corporate roles. When this campaign debuted in the United States in 2014, there was a rise in applications for corporate employment, and the campaign was expanded to the United Kingdom as a result of its success. Furthermore, Starbucks conducts ethical coffee procurement and has sought to promote local agricultural programs through their regional branches across the world.

8

# CONFLICT RESOLUTION

If you work with others, you will almost certainly encounter the need for conflict resolution at some point. You may be called upon to mediate a disagreement between members of your team or department. Or you might be enraged by something a colleague allegedly said about or to you in a meeting. Alternatively, you may need to mediate a disagreement with a client over a missed deadline. Conflict is unavoidable in organizations, and good conflict resolution tools are essential.

Conflict resolution is the process by which two or more parties reach a peaceful resolution to their dispute. It can be an informal or formal process.

There are several emotional and cognitive traps, most of which are unconscious and can aggravate conflict and contribute to the need for conflict resolution:

- **Self-serving interpretations of fairness.** Instead of deciding what is fair from a neutral standpoint, we decide what is fair from a personal standpoint and then justify this as fairness. Managers, for example, are likely

to believe their departments are entitled to a big share of the annual budget. Conflicts arise when people disagree about what is fair from their point of view.
- **Excessive self-assurance.** We have a tendency to be overconfident in our judgments, which leads to unrealistic expectations. Parties to a dispute, for instance, are likely to be overconfident in their chances of winning a lawsuit, which can lead them to reject a negotiated settlement that would save them time and money.
- **Commitment escalation.** Even long after their course of action has proven useful, negotiators are prone to irrationally increase their commitment to it. This applies in any conflict situation—a merger, a disagreement with a coworker or a labor strike, their chosen course of action long after it has proven useful.

We desperately try to recoup our previous investments in a dispute, failing to recognize that such costs should have no bearing on our future decisions.

- **Avoidance of conflict.** We may try to suppress negative emotions in the hope that they will fade with time because they cause us discomfort and distress. The truth is, conflict becomes more entrenched when parties avoid dealing with their strong emotions, leading to an even stronger need for conflict resolution.

## CAUSES OF CONFLICT IN THE WORKPLACE

Conflict in the workplace can take many forms, from insults to bullying to refusal to cooperate. The negative consequences of such actions can include decreased productivity, emotional stress, absenteeism, and a generally negative and toxic work environment for all—including for those who are not party to the conflict. It goes without saying that resolving workplace conflict is critical.

When conflicts arise, managers need to have the presence of mind to distinguish substance from noise and guide their teams away from ego-driven emotions toward places of mutuality and shared goals.

The causes of workplace conflict vary, but experts identify a few common ones that are worth mentioning.

**Ineffective Communication**

Poor communication from management or between employees can lead to misinformation, comments made out of context, and rumors. This is one of the most common causes of workplace conflict among employees.

**Clashes in values and personality**

Conflicts can arise when people fail to recognize and accept differences or understand others. In today's diverse and inclusive work environments, it's even more important for team members to respect one another's differences.

**Excessive workloads and inadequate resources**

Team members may feel resentment toward their manager if they feel they are being pushed too hard to perform or their workload is unmanageable. This may result in conflict.

In some situations, team members may feel like they are set up for failure when there aren't enough resources in the organization. When organizations don't have adequate resources for employees to do their jobs, pressure to compete for those resources can arise.

**Uncertainty about roles and responsibilities**

Team members may find themselves stepping on each other's toes if job descriptions and roles are unclear. When job descriptions are not clear, people become confused because there is uncertainty as to who does what. People ultimately start blaming one another when things start falling through the cracks.

## LEVELS OF CONFLICT

When dealing with people from diverse origins, personalities, and opinions, you may encounter conflict. Resolving disagreement, on the other hand, may bring up great chances for open dialogue, growth, and improved relationships.

Understanding the different forms of workplace conflict will help you choose the best way to resolve them. There are different levels of conflict that can influence a person or a group of people.

Each level has its own set of obstacles and solutions. The four degrees of conflict are as follows:

*Intrapersonal Conflict*

This level refers to an internal conflict involving only one person. This disagreement stems from your own thoughts, feelings, beliefs, values, and predispositions. It might happen when you're trying to decide between what you "want to do" and what you "should do."

For example: Sherry is looking to add a new member to her sales team. She examines numerous candidates and believes that three of them would make good sales reps, but she is unsure which one to select. She puts off hiring for a month while she thinks about it.

When dealing with intrapersonal conflict:

- **Stay true to your values.** Determine how the disagreement affects your basic values and what is important to your working efficiency. Consider alternatives that are consistent with your core ideals and goals.
- **Examine your organization's policies.** Examine the corporate policies that pertain to the disagreement, if appropriate. Follow any existing processes or seek direction from a supervisor.
- **Make a note of the dispute.** Examine the pros and drawbacks of the disagreement and forecast the effects of the different options. Consider choosing the resolution with the most benefits or the best outcomes.
- **Keep an eye on the clock.** Consider how much time you have to find a solution. Consider setting a deadline to ensure that the disagreement is handled as soon as possible.

*Interpersonal Conflict*

In a broader organization, this is a dispute between two or more persons. It might be caused by distinct personalities or different viewpoints on how to achieve goals. Interpersonal conflict can even arise without one side being aware of it.

For example: Pamela has been a digital marketer at her organization for four years and has always expected to take over as director of marketing when the current one retires. When it came time to fill the position, however, the organization recruited another employee who had only been with the organization for a year. Pamela was dissatisfied with both her previous and new supervisors, but she never expressed her sentiments to any of them.

Here are four actions you may take to manage workplace interpersonal conflict:

- **Identify the dispute.** Begin by determining the specific nature of the disagreement, including what incident precipitated it and how each side reacted to the circumstances. Examine the problem from each side's perspective to establish what each party wants and requires from the resolution.
- **Place the conflict in context.** Discuss the effects of the disagreement on each person, the project, and the workplace. This phase can help each side grasp the significance of resolving the problem and inspire them to work together to find a solution.
- **Create alternatives.** Allow each person to come up with one suggestion to fix the problem, taking turns. This phase allows each side to determine how to resolve the problem amicably. Parties can also collaborate to develop solutions that benefit all parties.
- **Determine a solution.** Figure out a solution that benefits each stakeholder as a group. Consider integrating goal-setting as part of this stage to evaluate and track the progress of a resolution.

*Intragroup Conflict*

When there are several people with various viewpoints, backgrounds, and experiences working toward a shared objective, this kind of conflict arises amongst members of a single group. Even though they all desire to attain the same objective, they may disagree on how to get there. Intragroup conflict can also arise when team members' communication methods and personalities clash.

For example: Jane and Shirley think that a direct mail campaign to a certain audience is the ideal marketing plan for the launch of a new product. William and Shaun feel that using social media advertisements is a superior strategy. Ashley feels that an influencer campaign would be the most effective. Because of the dispute, no promotional plan has been developed, despite the fact that the launch date is just two weeks away. Tensions are high, and the delays are affecting other departments.

Here are three actions you may take to efficiently manage intragroup conflicts:

- **As a group, discuss the conflict.** Discuss openly what sparked the dispute and how each side feels about it. This phase guarantees that everyone is involved in coming up with a solution and may discuss the problem openly. Allow each team member to explain why they hold their opinion and provide the material that supports these ideas.
- **Work together in small groups.** Divide the team into smaller groups with various perspectives. Analyze the conflict and discuss the benefits and drawbacks of various solutions. Gather as a team and have groups discuss their thoughts. Smaller groups can give more in-depth talks, since fewer individuals are trying to argue their point at the same time.
- **Reach a consensus as a team.** Decide what course of action to follow as a group or whether further brainstorming is required. Ascertain that everyone is happy with the choice and committed to the planned strategy.

*Intergroup Conflict*

This type of conflict arises between distinct groups within a bigger organization or between those who do not share common aims.

For example: An e-commerce organization's marketing staff is advertising a brand-new project that is expected to boost each average order value by 15%. They develop a timetable and notify clients of the launch date. Despite their best efforts, the web developers in charge of building and deploying the additional functionality on the website are running behind schedule. The web developers are annoyed by unrealistic timelines, while the marketing department is unhappy about the launch's delay.

Here are three simple steps to get you started:

1. **Discuss the matter with all parties involved.** You can converse with huge groups, such as in an open forum. This circumstance may be appropriate for issues affecting a large number of people and may be utilized to hear a range of opinions, ideas, and concerns from a smaller group of stakeholders.
2. **Hold a confidential meeting with all relevant parties.** Address an intergroup disagreement with only a few key persons, such as team leaders or department heads, at a time. This stage might follow after an open forum or as the primary settlement strategy.
3. **Collect a range of potential solutions.** Encourage both parties to meet to discuss concerns as they occur. If feasible, shift team members from one team to another so they may see an issue from the other team's point of view. Then, organize groups to develop alternatives that will have the greatest beneficial impact. Consider taking

a vote to evaluate each side's interest in the offered solutions in order to reach an agreement.

While these steps can be used to handle various degrees of conflict, consider the following suggestions to assist you in managing workplace conflict in a range of situations:

**Set a suitable meeting time and location**

Request that everyone concerned set aside some time to address the problem. Find a quiet, comfortable place where you may speak freely and without interruption.

**Maintain your cool and be specific**

Maintain your cool throughout the discussion and attempt to concentrate on practical outcomes. Discuss specifics of a disagreement so that they may be handled freely.

**Make use of active listening**

Consider paraphrasing the other person's viewpoint to demonstrate that you understand their concerns and issues. If you are mediating the disagreement, this stage might assist you and the entire group to comprehend what is going on.

**Celebrate your progress and accomplishments**

Acknowledge each team members' efforts toward a behavioral change, attitude, or approach. When the team achieves goals as a result of the resolution, recognize and celebrate those accomplishments.

## SIGNS OF CONFLICT IN THE TEAM

Conflict does not arise out of nothing. There are usually signals that a confrontation is brewing. Managers who recognize these warning indicators can be proactively engaging the issue before it escalates. Remember that anything that prevents optimal productivity and pleasant connection between employees and management is a clear indicator that all is not well and needs to be handled before it gets out of hand.

Here are the most common signs of conflict in the workplace:

- **Meetings that are dysfunctional.** Do staff meetings devolve into squabbles rather than brainstorming sessions? Do certain people always seem to dominate the discussion while others look irritated or distracted?
- **Seemingly unprovoked outbursts.** Any anger, especially if it is an overreaction, must be handled quickly. Anger is rarely the appropriate reaction to a first-time upset.
- **Productivity declines.** When people are dissatisfied with their workplace, they tend to focus less on their work. Consider whether there has been a decrease in your team's productivity and attempt to determine when it began.
- **Staff turnover has increased.** There is a legitimate reason why employees are leaving. Nobody loves looking for work; therefore, the fact that individuals are leaving suggests that there is an underlying problem.
- **Communications that are inappropriate.** This might take the shape of impolite or improper language in emails. Rudeness in words or contempt for another's perspective are signs that something is about to blow up.

- **Anxiety.** Is there somebody who appears worried or tense most of the time? Perhaps they avoid social encounters, constantly mistrust their job, or ask more questions than usual. Anxiety is frequently a sign that there is a problem developing on an interpersonal level.
- **Formation of cliques.** Employees should collaborate as a group. If there appears to be a separation into cliques or if the same personnel constantly seem to team up on projects, the firm isn't working as a whole and isn't being as productive as it could be.
- **Disagreements that occur repeatedly.** Is it common for the same personnel to disagree? Is the disagreement frequently about little matters? There is a communication problem that must be addressed promptly.
- **Lack of trust among team members.** Trust is crucial in every workplace, whether between coworkers or between coworkers and management. If there appears to be mistrust inside the organization, it must be addressed.

If you notice these or other signs that trouble is brewing among your employees, do not assume that the problem will go away on its own; the situation must be addressed as soon as possible by you or HR staff. In many cases, a professional conflict advisor can assist everyone in identifying the root cause of the conflict and resolving any issues.

HOW TO RESOLVE CONFLICT IN THE WORKPLACE

Here are some steps that will help you find resolutions to conflict in the workplace or your team:

### Understand what the conflict is about

Before you start communicating with the other party, make sure you fully understand your position in the conflict as well as the other party's position. It's also critical to define your own and the other person's interests. Consider what you truly care about in the conflict, what your concerns are, and what you would like to see happen. Repeat the exercise, but this time consider the conflict from the other party's point of view. Consider what kinds of agreements you might be able to reach.

### Investigate alternatives

In some cases, the parties to a conflict are unable to reach an amicable resolution. You must consider this before sitting down with the other party to resolve the issue. Consider when you will leave the conflict and what you will do if you cannot reach an agreement. When you're brainstorming possible conflict resolutions, you can quickly compare each of those solutions to the best alternative that you've already decided on and determine if the new solution is better.

### Find a neutral, quiet location

It's critical to find a quiet, neutral location where you can talk about the conflict privately. Because the ultimate goal is to relieve tension, a private setting is essential. If you can close the doors and speak privately without being interrupted, a manager's office or even a conference room may work well.

### Communicate with both parties

It's time to communicate directly with one another after you've considered your own and the other party's interests and found a private, neutral location where you can speak. Here are some ideas to help you make the most of your time together:

- **Listen attentively.** Actively listen, rephrasing the statement in your own words to ensure you fully comprehend what the other party is saying. For example, you could begin with, "So you're saying…" or "Did I get you correctly?"
- **Allow everyone to participate.** Allow everyone who wants to contribute to the conversation to do so if there are multiple parties involved. Participants will have a say in how the conflict is resolved and will aid in the discovery of a solution.
- **Assumptions should be avoided.** Maintain an open mind, asking questions and gathering information to fully understand each position.
- **Maintain your cool.** Maintain your cool even if the other person becomes emotional. You may even want to apologize if necessary, as this can help to diffuse the situation.
- **Be mindful of your body language.**

Be aware of your body language, as you are communicating information to the other party without even speaking. You want to exude calmness and openness. Here are some examples:

- Maintain eye contact.
- Be aware of how you express yourself.
- Relax your neck and shoulders.
- Use a neutral tone at a medium speed and volume.
- Avoid words such as 'always' or 'never.'
- Determine a common goal.
- **Agree on next steps.**

Both parties agree on the desired outcome of the conflict in this step. After everyone has moved past the root cause of the problem, they frequently discover that they are all working toward the same goal, they just have different ideas about how to get there. Discuss what you want to see happen and your personal interests. Request that the other party do the same. You can begin working on a resolution once you've identified the common goal.

**Make use of a third-party mediator**

In some cases, using a neutral third party whom everyone trusts to be fair may be beneficial. This can help ensure that both parties fully understand one another and, if necessary, remind everyone of the overall goal so that the conversation and brainstorming session remains productive. The following are some possible jobs for the mediator:

- listening to both sides and explaining their respective positions
- identifying shared interests
- maintaining both parties' focus, respect, and reasonableness
- seeking solutions that are a win-win situation for both parties
- **Consider your options.**

Now that you have a thorough understanding of the conflict, the interests of each party, and the common goal of all parties, you can consider potential solutions. Make an effort to generate as many ideas as possible. Look for win-win solutions or compromises that can be agreed upon by all parties.

Discuss each concept. Consider what's at stake and whether the idea involves anyone else who should be consulted. If an idea cannot be implemented, explain why. If the conflict is between you and a subordinate, use their ideas first to increase their personal commitment and make them feel heard.

**Make a plan of action**

Determine which solutions you and the other party can accept and where you can find common ground. Ideally, you would find a solution that benefits everyone involved. If this isn't possible, look for an idea to which everyone can agree and commit.

# 9

# STRATEGIC PLANNING AND IMPLEMENTATION

Strategic planning is one of the most important management roles. It refers to the development of specific business plans, implementing them, and analyzing the results in relation to the organization's overarching long-term goals. Effective planning makes it possible for an organization to achieve goals. Furthermore, it enables teams to function smoothly and more effectively.

## PROCESS OF STRATEGIC PLANNING

The primary goal of the planning process is to assist organizations in setting goals and developing an actionable plan to achieve those goals. Strategic planning can occur at any level of an organization. There may be a plan in place that covers the goals of the entire organization, but there may also be plans designed and implemented by individual managers with their teams.

Strategic planning is critical to an organization's long-term success. A strategic plan allows an organization to focus its energies and resources on effectively achieving a goal.

The following steps will assist you in developing effective, actionable strategic plans:

## 1. Recognize and acknowledge the need for a strategic plan

Before the process of strategic planning begins, there needs to be a recognition and acknowledgment of the need for a strategic plan. This means as a manager, you must know and have a clear understanding of the environment and industry in which your organization operates in order to identify opportunities for growth. You must also be familiar with the organization's internal operations in order to recognize when a problem arises.

After you've identified opportunities, you can start thinking about actions that will help you capitalize on those opportunities. For example, the government could be offering contracts to companies in your industry and if you are aware of this, you can devise a strategy to help your organization compete.

## 2. Set objectives

Goals can be set for the organization as a whole or individual departments, depending on their purpose. Continuing with the government contract bid example, an organization-wide goal could be to secure the bid. In the meantime, a department goal might be to improve specific performance metrics, such as customer satisfaction or sales.

A goal for an organization can be broad, but when setting goals for a department, you must be specific and as detailed as possible so that your team members understand what is expected of them. For example, an organization-wide goal may be increasing profits, but individual departments will require more detailed profit-related goals, such as "By May 30, we will generate an additional $5,000 in revenue."

Goals are essential in strategic planning because they make it possible for managers to direct their teams more effectively. They provide team members with a common goal to work toward, making their daily activities more focused.

### 3. Create premises or assumptions

A strategic plan is a forecast of the future, and that should be kept in mind when developing one. Because the future is unpredictable, your plan must be based on certain assumptions or premises.

A forecast is a premise in which certain assumptions and predictions about the future are made. If the organization's goal is to increase profits, management must forecast whether or not, based on the conditions prevailing, the industry can support a profit increase.

You'll need to develop both internal and external premises during the strategic planning process. Internal premises are based on the organization's inner workings and factors. Internal premises examples include:

- the resources you anticipate having available
- organizational policies that you must or will be required to implement
- how the levels of management will interact with the plan

External premises are defined as anything outside of the organization that may have an impact on the plan and ability to meet set objectives. External premises examples include:

- the social and political climate
- developments in technology
- competition from organizations in the same industry

When attempting to achieve an organizational goal, it is critical that all managers operate under the same premises and agree on the premises.

**4. Investigate various approaches to achieving goals**

There are a number of approaches to achieving a goal. You must devote time to researching various ways your team could collaborate to achieve a specific goal. It is important for managers to look into the different methods available to them that will help in achieving that goal. With a number of different methods at their disposal, they will have a level of flexibility when directing their teams. Some managers may prefer to use innovative solutions to achieve goals, whereas others may prefer to use conventional methods.

The purpose of researching different approaches is to enable managers to come up with a few most suitable and viable options that will allow them to effectively achieve their goals.

When you've identified a few viable potential solutions to your problems, you need to thoroughly examine each one to determine which is the best option. You must consider each option's weaknesses and strengths, especially as they relate to your organization's goals. Let's say you are creating a financial plan for the organization; you would need to evaluate the potential risks and returns for each possible plan. You would also need to evaluate each option to see if it would help you achieve your ultimate goal more efficiently.

### 5. Choose your course of action

With the objective set, assumptions developed and identified, and different solutions for completing your goals, you can direct your attention to making a decision on the best course of action to take. Before choosing your plan of action, consider the following:

- Steer clear of options that could end up costing the organization money in both the short or long term.
- Go with the plan with the fewest potential adverse consequences. Every plan has advantages and disadvantages, but some plans have more disadvantages than others. Compare the various options for achieving your goal and select the one with the best chance of success.
- Choose a plan of action that is flexible and adaptable. While carrying out your strategy, you may encounter unexpected challenges. A flexible plan will allow you to maneuver and overcome these obstacles more easily if your plan is flexible than if it is fixed. For example, if your organization is working on a government contract bid and the government implements a new policy, you may need to make some adjustments to your bid to comply with the new policy.
- When developing a strategic plan, you should rely on solid evidence; for instance, mathematical analysis. Your experience as a manager can also help you decide which plan is best for achieving your goals. Using your personal experience, you may realize that one of the plans under consideration is similar to something you have seen implemented before and know to be effective.

You can also take elements from different strategic plans and combine them in your plan. For example, if you compare two financial plans, one may have a better solution for increasing profits and the other may have an effective strategy for protecting the business from unexpected losses. A combination of these two elements can form a solid plan.

**6. Create a backup plan**

Once you've decided on which plan to implement, you may need to create a plan to aid in the implementation of the primary plan. This secondary plan will differ depending on your goals, so keep them in mind as you develop it.

If your organization's goal is to launch a new product, your main plan may include steps such as product research, manufacturing arrangements, and developing a marketing strategy. The secondary plan will include all of the steps required to support the implementation of the primary plan.

Continuing with the product launch example, if you need to expand your product research team, the appointment of new people could be a step in your backup plan. Similarly, if your organization does not already have a product research team, you may need to hire one or, if your organization's manufacturing facilities are not suitable for the manufacturing of the new product, you may need to increase your manufacturing capability. Regardless of the goal, training the people who will implement it is a common component of a secondary plan. Whether you are attempting to launch a new product or increase sales of an existing product, your employees will most likely require additional training before the organization can achieve these goals.

**7. Put the strategic plan into action**

Putting the plan into action is the last step in the strategic planning process. This is usually the most involved step in the planning process. When it comes time to put a plan into action, managers rely on their experience and skill set to ensure that everything goes smoothly.

Managers must take the time to ensure that their team members understand how they fit into the larger picture and their roles, if the organizational goal is particularly complex. All team members must be informed and collaborate to ensure the project's success.

The tools required to carry out the plan will vary depending on the circumstances. If, for example, your plan involves changing a policy, the legal department will have to be consulted at implementation to ensure that the policy is properly outlined and effective.

## STRATEGY IMPLEMENTATION

Now that the strategic plan is in place, it needs to be implemented. Strategy implementation is the process of putting plans into action to achieve a specific goal. It is the part where the plan is put into action and brought to life. Every organization's success is dependent on its ability to implement decisions and execute key processes effectively, efficiently, and consistently. What steps can you take to ensure that a strategy is implemented successfully?

A successfully executed and implemented strategy is one that delivers what's planned on budget, on time, and is of the expected quality with minimum variability. Even the best-laid plans may fail if the implementation process is inefficient.

As a manager looking to implement strategic change in your organization, follow these seven steps to successfully introduce and roll out a new strategy.

### 1. Define key variables and set clear goals

The first thing is to identify the objectives that the new strategy is intended to achieve. If there's no clear picture of what you want to achieve, it can be difficult to devise a strategy for getting there.

Setting goals that are impossible to achieve is a common mistake when it comes to professional development, business, or even personal development. Remember that your objectives should be attainable. Setting unrealistic goals can leave you and your team feeling uninspired, overwhelmed, potentially burned out, and deflated.

Review the performances and outcomes—both the successes and failures—of previous change initiatives to determine what's realistic given your time frame and resources. Use your previous experience to define what success entails.

It's also important to account for variables that may impede your team's ability to achieve them and develop contingency plans; this is a critical aspect of goal-setting. The better prepared you are, the more likely the implementation will be successful.

### 2. Establish responsibilities, roles, and relationships

Once you've determined your goals and the variables that may stand in your way, you should create a roadmap for achieving those goals, set expectations for your team, and clearly communicate how the implementation plan works to avoid confusion.

During this stage, it can be beneficial to document all of the available resources, including the teams, individual employees, and departments that will be involved. Outline a clear picture of what each resource is accountable for, and establish a process that everyone should follow when communicating on matters relating to the project.

Implementing strategic plans necessitates solid relationships.

As a manager, it will be your responsibility not only to tell people who the decision-makers are, who is accountable for what, and what to do when an unforeseen issue arises, but also the process to be followed when interacting with one another and how often.

### 3. Assign work

Determine who needs to do what, once you've determined what needs to be done to ensure success. Refer to your original timeline and goal list, and assign tasks to team members as needed.

Explain the big picture idea to your team so that they understand the organization's vision, and ensure that everyone is aware of their specific responsibilities. To avoid overwhelming individual team members, set deadlines. Remember to resist the temptation to micromanage; your job as a manager is to keep your team focused and achieve goals.

### 4. Execute, track performance and progress, and provide ongoing assistance

After assigning work, put the plan into action. One of the most difficult skills to learn as a manager is how to effectively support and guide their team members. While your primary focus will most likely be delegation, it is critical that you make yourself available to answer questions or address challenges and roadblocks that your team may encounter.

Check in on your team's progress on a regular basis and listen to their feedback.

Using daily, weekly, and monthly status reports and check-ins to provide updates, re-establishing due dates and milestones, and ensuring all teams are aligned is one effective strategy for tracking progress.

### 5. Be nimble—revise and adjust as necessary

Because implementation is an iterative process, the work does not end when you believe you have reached your goal. Processes can change in the middle, and challenges or unexpected issues can come up. As the nature of the project changes, your original objectives may need to shift.

It is more important to be alert, flexible, and willing to change or readjust plans as you supervise implementation than it is to stick rigidly to your original goals.

On a regular basis, you need to ask yourself and your team, "Do we need to adjust?" If so, how so? Do we have to start from scratch? The answers to these questions can be extremely useful.

### 6. Obtain project closure and agreement on output

Based on the goals established at the outset, everyone on the team should agree on what the final product should look like. When the strategy is successfully implemented, find out if each department and team member has everything they need to finish the job and are satisfied with their work.

Gather details, information, and results from your team in preparation for your report to your management team. These will help you to paint an accurate picture of the project and processes.

### 7. Perform a review of the project and process

Once implementation is completed, take a step back and assess how things went. Consider the following:

- Did we meet our objectives? If not, why not? What steps must we take to achieve our objectives?
- What obstacles or challenges arose during the project that could have been anticipated? How can we avoid such difficulties in the future?
- What general lessons can we draw from the process?

While failure is never the goal, a flawed or unsuccessful strategy implementation can be a valuable learning experience for an organization if time is spent understanding what went wrong and why.

Successful strategy implementation can be difficult, and it necessitates strong management and leadership abilities. Effective delegation, emotional intelligence, patience, communication skills, and thorough organizational abilities are essential.

Consider taking a leadership or management course that aligns with your professional as well as personal goals if you want to improve your skills and become a better manager. Management training courses are frequently designed to be flexible, but they provide critical, hands-on learning opportunities from leading industry experts that can be applied to any profession.

10

# SETTING KEY PERFORMANCE INDICATORS

Organizations and businesses are constantly looking for ways to enhance their operations and performance. They frequently use performance measurements to discover major improvement possibilities that will assist them to meet market needs.

Key performance indicators (KPIs) may assist your organization in measuring internal processes, activities, and productivity in order to achieve certain goals or objectives. KPIs connect organizational vision to individual behavior. In an ideal world, KPIs would cascade from level to level within an organization. You can visualize this by thinking of your organization as a pyramid.

These indicators can assist the organization in identifying areas for improvement as well as areas where it thrives. KPIs are also significant for the following reasons:

**Improve staff morale**

Motivating employees and increasing job happiness might help your firm perform better. It may also promote a good and collaborative culture inside your business. KPIs tell employees how they are performing as individuals, as a team, and as a firm. Positive feedback may boost motivation and encourage productive behavior to continue.

### Help the organization's goals

Because they report on the organization's operations, workers, and financial performance, comprehensive KPI measuring tools may assist and promote an organization's business objectives. Implementing KPI metrics that target each critical component of the business can boost the chance of the firm meeting its objectives. For example, if an organization's aim is to acquire 30 new customer accounts by the end of the year, adding a KPI that monitors the number of client accounts gained each month can assist the company in tracking and meeting its objectives.

### Encourage business expansion

Organizations that properly use KPI tools are able to support employee and corporate growth. This is because it may uncover opportunities for improvement and assist a firm in identifying continuous improvement projects. It may also show employees what talents they might build to assist and enhance their work performance.

### Control organization performance

Access to KPI reporting assists each member in maintaining personal, team, and department responsibility. Individual responsibility can help to improve communication and create positive performance. Furthermore, it promotes transparency by analyzing qualitative or quantitative data rather than depending on people to track and report their own performance.

**Progress should be measured**

Implementing KPI measures can also assist an organization in tracking its progress and improvements. Using KPI reports to calculate an average performance value can help you when doing comparisons. It can also help determine whether the existing processes and policies are working to improve operations.

**Examine trends**

KPI reports also help businesses identify negative and positive performance trends. This can assist businesses in quickly identifying and implementing measures to help mitigate negative trends. These reports also make it possible for an organization to get a better idea of which processes are assisting them in their success and which are not.

An organization can incorporate several KPI management tools into their operations to provide current insight into their business. Among the various KPI types are:

**Financial metrics**

Adding financial management tools to track expenses, cash flows, and sales throughout the month can help businesses quickly identify any issues that need to be addressed. This also helps to keep minor issues from becoming larger hurdles to overcome. Some businesses use KPI tools to track supply costs, daily expenses, or customer invoices in order to accurately track the organization's financial operations.

## Employee evaluations

Tracking employee data can assist in identifying performance issues or areas for improvement. Organizations frequently analyze employee hours, overtime hours, and project statuses to determine employee productivity. This can also give you ideas on how to increase productivity by allocating projects differently or adjusting employee hours.

## Operational controls

Operational measures enable businesses to track the quality and efficiency of their operations. These metrics may look at product quality, supplier quality, and machine output. By analyzing and implementing these measures, you'll be able to assist your organization to identify operational challenges and incorporate modified or new processes to overcome those challenges.

### CHOOSING THE RIGHT KPIS

There are several factors to consider when selecting key performance indicators that are appropriate for your organization. In some cases, a combination of measures may be used to achieve your organization's objectives. Consider the following four steps to help you choose the best KPI:

1. **Establish company procedures**

When deciding which KPI methods to implement in your organization, consider the business practices you want to improve first. If you want to improve your financial situation, consider using financial KPIs instead of employee indicators. This can help to ensure that your organization is actively measuring progress and working toward financial objectives.

**2. Determine the process requirements**

Determining what a KPI should measure before implementing the process can ensure that your company receives reports with actionable results. Furthermore, each KPI should assist a company in achieving its overall goals and objectives.

**3. Include outcome measurements**

Each KPI should ideally provide results that your company can analyze and use to create new or updated processes. All parties involved in your company's improvement strategies should be able to easily analyze the data in the report. This can assist more employees in providing relevant input to improve your organization's operations.

**Processes should be adjusted**

It's also critical for your organization to determine if a KPI is not adding value or delivering the desired results. Making sure you can adapt or adjust your KPIs to meet the organization's needs can help you prove that these metrics are beneficial to your organization. Furthermore, getting rid of a specific KPI measure can help prevent data surplus, which prevents your organization from focusing on relevant data.

## IMPLEMENTING KPIS EFFECTIVELY

Organizations employ a unique set of KPIs to assess various processes, performance, and productivity. Here are some things to think about when implementing these measures in your organization:

**Ascertain that the KPIs are attainable, actionable, and measurable**

Providing measures that your organization can achieve in a specific time frame can assist you in analyzing the organization's progress toward the goal. Furthermore, ensuring that you can measure progress can provide you with accurate insight into the performance indicators.

**Regularly assess effectiveness**

Setting timelines for reevaluating and adjusting KPIs can help ensure that your organization is constantly improving. It also assists your organization in making consistent progress toward its revenue, sales, or performance goals.

**Maintain consistency in KPIs**

Maintaining consistent KPIs can help your organization stay on track and avoid confusion. This stability can also assist those in charge of improvement projects in quickly analyzing and determining progress.

## DEVELOPING SMART KPIS

Whatever the nature of your KPIs is, you must ensure that they are SMART. This concept is similar to the one discussed in Chapter 5 when we were talking about setting goals, but it's important that we repeat what SMART stands for as it pertains to KPIs.

**Specific:** Specify what each KPI will measure and why it is important.

**Measurable:** The KPI must be measurable in comparison to a predefined standard.

**Attainable:** You must be able to meet the KPI.

**Relevant:** Your KPI must measure something that is important and helps to improve performance.

**Time-Bound:** The KPI must be completed within a specified time frame.

When you complete a KPI, it should meet all of the SMART criteria. For example, "Increase new paid sign-ups to the website by 25% by the end of the second quarter of the fiscal year."

To help you understand the context and define effective KPIs, ask yourself the following questions:

- What is the vision of your organization? What is the plan for realizing that vision?
- Which metrics will show that you are on track with your vision and strategy?
- How many metrics do you need?
- What should you use as a yardstick?
- How could the metrics be manipulated, and how will you prevent this?

*Managing Your KPIs*

When deciding which KPIs to implement, consider how you will collect the necessary data. Net profit, for example, necessitates a different set of data than customer satisfaction and access to different systems. Determine who will collect the data and how frequently. Sales data, for example, can usually be collected daily, whereas KPIs that require data from multiple sources may be better measured weekly or monthly.

You must also verify the data to ensure that it is accurate and meets all of the requirements of your KPI. Communicate KPIs clearly to all parties involved. Make sure your team understands how each KPI affects their work and which activities to prioritize.

11

# MANAGING CHANGE

Managers can either be a valuable contributor to successful change or a formidable impediment. The ability of managers to lead their teams through change is frequently the deciding factor in how completely and quickly a change is adopted.

Change is an essential component of all organizations and businesses; it is how they evolve and grow to become more successful. It is critical for those who implement change to ensure the process moves along as smoothly and quickly as possible. Implementing change management effectively is essential in making it possible for employees to achieve a common goal of helping an organization advance as a whole.

Change management refers to the various methods by which an organization prepares for and implements change. The majority of change management implementations are concerned with how employees accept and adapt to new ways of doing things. Whether the change is simple or complex, the primary goal is to ensure that it brings the organization closer to its goals.

Change management can be applied to almost any aspect of workplace change. Changes to business processes, resource utilization, operational tactics, and budgeting used in your organization's day-to-day operations are examples. It can also refer to personal changes, such as training and promoting an employee to take on a larger role with more responsibility within your organization.

## CHANGE MANAGEMENT LEVELS

Change management is classified into three types. It is critical to understand these categories in order to implement change management in an effective manner on an organizational and individual level.

**Personal change management**

The success of new procedures or policies in the workplace begins with and is determined by the people who make up the company. Individual change management necessitates an understanding of what motivates people to change and how this can be incorporated into day-to-day business operations. You must consider what processes to implement in order to make your team more willing to accept a change in their roles or tasks.

**Managing change that involves teams across the organization**

Individuals, obviously, play an important role in any change, and considering long-term goals is an important part of implementing long-term change throughout an organization. Organizational change management is frequently used as part of project management to ensure that the solutions developed during the project are implemented permanently. This could include pinpointing the teams that the change will impact the most, informing them of how they'll be affected by the change, and then training them on how to implement the change properly.

**Change management when the organization changes**

This level of change management completely restructures an organization. It has an impact on leadership, policies, processes, projects, roles, procedures, and organizational structure. If you are planning an enterprise change program, you will need acceptance from all levels of your organization. This will give you more freedom to create a new business that is tailored to your organization's objectives.

TYPES OF ORGANIZATIONAL CHANGE

An organization may go through several types of change, all of which can be better managed through change management procedures. Knowing what kind of change your company is going through or needs can help you decide which change management method to use.

The following are examples of common organizational changes:

- **Developmental change:** This type of change can include any improvement to how an organization currently operates.
- **Transitional change:** A transitional change occurs when a business enters a new state of being. When one organization merges with another, this is an example of transitional change.
- **Transformational change:** This is the most drastic type of change within a business. It occurs when an organization decides to overhaul its current business model. For example, an organization may launch new products that are unlike anything it has previously created or was previously known for.

## MANAGING CHANGE

Managing organizational change is a difficult task. Leaders must align people with the reason for the change, which often means going against long-held habits and beliefs. Organizations are more likely to succeed when change initiatives are planned ahead of time and employees are engaged before, during, and after the change. The following are seven strategies for effective change management in organizations.

### 1. Prioritize people

People are prioritized in successful change management. People drive change and keep it going. When the people involved do not understand, believe in, or participate in the change, the initiative fails.

Leaders facilitate change by involving employees in the process. Leaders achieve this through proactive change management communication, which fosters a desire for change throughout the workforce. If people do not believe in the change and are not motivated by others to act, change initiatives will fail.

### 2. Use a change management model

When it comes to implementing change, leaders must contend with company culture, organizational momentum, and human psychology. They need the right tools to guide them in order to effect change. Change management models assist leaders in linking business strategy to action, increasing the likelihood of success.

There are several change management models to choose from (for example, Lewin's Change Management Model, Prosci's ADKAR model, and Kotter's Change Management Model). Each model differs, but they all adhere to the core tenants of identifying needs, planning for change, and implementation.

### 3. Employees can be empowered through communication

Communication is a critical component of successfully managing organizational change. A change in vision is only as effective as the communication that supports it. Effective change management communication clarifies why the change is required and mobilizes employees with a sense of urgency to implement the change. When businesses fail to communicate, they fail to drive meaningful change.

Change management communication is not a one-time information transfer. It necessitates dedication, consistency, and clarity. Employees should be engaged through two-way communication methods such as focus groups, surveys and informal feedback collection. Employees feel valued when leadership involves them. Employees who feel valued are more likely to embrace change and contribute to its implementation.

Two-way communication makes it possible for leaders to identify any barriers to change and address them before they become a problem. Proactive action by leaders can enable the organization to respond to issues that could possibly lead to problems, thus averting resistance to change.

### 4. Activate leadership

The success of change management initiatives is dependent on visible and active leadership participation.

**5. Make change interesting and exciting**

Communication that is clear, purposeful, and consistent results in people having a better understanding of the rationale behind a change. This targeted communication strategy provides context for understanding the change's what, why, and so what. Effective communication answers the most important question that people have: What does this mean to me, and how will it affect my work? Employees who have a better understanding of the change are much more likely to ask, "How can I help make this happen?"

Transformation that happens when people are genuinely engaged and believe in the vision is so much more profound than one where employees just go with the flow and don't engage. Strong employee support discourages change resistance, which could stymie the organization.

**6. Keep an eye out for high and low points in momentum**

During change initiatives, there will be both high and low points. Leaders can manage and leverage these points in time proactively. Leaders should celebrate victories during times of transition to keep momentum going. Leaders can reset communication strategies at low points to listen to employee input and build trust and support. Being proactive assists leaders in managing momentum for maximum success.

**7. Don't dismiss opposition**

Change resistance is poisonous to the transformation of an organization. When resistance is identified early, it is much easier to overcome. Leaders should be on the lookout for signs of change resistance such as inaction, procrastination, withholding information, and rumors.

People are at the heart of change, and they are the lifeblood of successful, growing organizations. Leaders position themselves and their organizations for effective organizational change management by proactively engaging employees and ensuring transparent, clear, and consistent communication.

## CHANGE MANAGEMENT MISTAKES TO AVOID

Change is the only constant, especially in the business world. Your job as a manager is to help your team navigate through change of any size, especially big changes. However, this is easier said than done, and managers find themselves making mistakes they could have easily avoided, if they knew how.

**Failing to develop a pre, during, and post change communication plan**

The leading problem when it comes to moving employees through change is insufficient communication. Employees are more accepting of change if the organization they work for practices transparency and provides sufficient information pre, during, and post the change process. Different forms of communication should take place at different times, and these should form part of a clear and detailed communication plan. It's safer to over communicate than to communicate inadequately or not at all. It's better to err on the side of caution. Furthermore, it is important that managers and leaders say the same thing; conflicting messages from leaders create confusion, uncertainty, fear, and, ultimately, resistance.

### Not taking seriously the underlying reasons for resistance

Assuming that resistance to change is due to difficult or disengaged employees is a mistake that leaders make. However, people tend not to buy into an idea they perceive to be bad. Employees, in most cases, resist change because the information they have tells them this initiative is ill-founded, unwise, or unlikely to work. Leaders need to take action on the true sources of resistance, but this can only happen if leaders take an active interest in discovering them.

### Implying the change is less serious than it really is

Leaders often give a simplistic perspective of the change and tend to miss its complexity. A leader needs to have the ability to see the impact of change across multiple systems in order to properly address the complexity of the changes.

### Failing to incorporate employee feedback and asking for it

Leaders need to constantly and consistently seek feedback when instituting change. This feedback should be on the real-time effects of the changes. Furthermore, leaders should be open to adjusting their plans to incorporate employee feedback, if that is what's necessary to achieve the desired results. The effects of change should be constantly measured, and managers should seek feedback from the affected team members. This data from the team members will help you make the required adjustments to get the best possible results.

### Failing to educate people about the change

Leaders have the tendency to dictate change instead of

educating their employees about it. Although instituting change top down is your prerogative, this is likely to backfire. People adapt and accept change when organizations bring the change gently. The best ways to create positive change include peer-to-peer education, training, and teaching.

**Leadership participation is not consistent**

Inconsistent leadership sponsorship is one of the biggest reasons for change initiatives not materializing or failing. With time change, leaders become inactive; however, they tend to be very vocal at the beginning of the process. The lack of visibility counters the success of the initiative and fuels more resistance. Leaders should not be visible just at the beginning, they should be visible and active throughout the change process.

**Expecting change to be accepted immediately**

People go through stages when processing major changes. Support your team through each phase and understand that acceptance or buy-in is a gradual process. Provide them with all the information they need to process their feelings and observe their reactions. Over and above, be available with answers to some of the questions they might have.

**Assuming employees know how to proceed**

Change leaders tend to set out what needs to happen but neglect to make sure employees know how to make those things happen. Many employees, perhaps feeling intimidated, will remain silent. Some become irritated and scared for their jobs. The organization must provide training to help employees develop their skills. Coaching programs can assist employees in identifying emotions that may be impeding their progress.

Change is inevitable and necessary for organizations to grow, but to employees, it may be frightening. You can smooth the transition for your employees and make the change stick if you have the correct communication techniques in place.

# CONCLUSION

Some people work their way up the corporate ladder, others are placed in management positions depending on company needs. Regardless of how you became a manager, for the first time, you have probably just found out that being a manager is a job unlike any. Nothing prepares you for a managerial position, and no one gives you training. You learn on the job every day. Everyone who has ever been a first-time manager will agree that continuous learning is essential for long-term success.

So, don't worry if you're having trouble managing a diverse group of people on your team. Everyone has to start somewhere, and it's better to start now than later.

Before you learn the basics of how to be a manager and a leader, it's important for you to understand that managing people is not synonymous with leadership, and the other way round. To some, these concepts are the same, but on close inspection, you will notice they are not. Where a leader asks "Why?" a manager will ask "How?" You can be both a leader and a manager, but you don't need to be a manager to be a leader. In Chapter 1, we discussed the

## CONCLUSION

qualities that both leaders and managers display, the difference between the two, as well as characteristics all effective managers have.

Managing people is what a manager does, and an effective manager knows the importance of having the ability to manage themselves. Managing people is a taxing job, and it's important that you learn to manage your time, stress levels, and health. Self-management skills are a must-have for a manager, because how can you manage others if you can't manage yourself?

In Chapter 3, we discussed the primary role of a manager—managing people. We talked at length about what you should know as a first-time manager and different styles of management, and we also covered some of the mistakes that new managers make and what to do to avoid making them.

Delegation is an important part of managing people and an indication of an effective manager. As a first-time manager, you will find the idea of delegating daunting because it will be a new concept to you. In Chapter 4, we covered delegation at length. To delegate effectively, you need to understand the strategies for effective delegation, types of delegation, and the dos and don'ts of delegation.

As a manager, goal-setting is important for keeping your team members focused and motivated. We discussed the common mistakes managers make when setting goals and we gave you a tool for setting goals that are simple, measurable, attainable, relevant and time-bound. As a manager you need to be able to measure the performance of your team against organizational goals and using the SMART approach. By setting proper goals, you're making sure your team succeeds.

In today's world, it's critical that your workforce is a reflection of society and that everyone is able to speak their minds and share ideas. As a manager, you need to be adequately equipped to deal with people of diverse cultures, backgrounds, genders, and reli-

CONCLUSION

gions. Managing diverse teams differs greatly from managing a homogeneous workforce. The content in Chapter 6 provided you with information and insight that will help you prepare yourself adequately. At the end of this chapter we discussed a few corporations that have made diversity and inclusion part of their corporate culture and have seen immense benefits.

People want to have a sense of purpose in their lives and their work. Purpose drives people to focus on their goals. A workforce whose purpose is aligned with that of the organization is a happy workforce. Furthermore, many organizations are adopting a business approach that is purpose-driven rather than profit-driven. For that reason, it is important for managers to embody that and have it reflect in how they manage their teams.

The workplace brings people from different opinions and beliefs together, and there is bound to be conflicts and misunderstanding. Managers are tasked with resolving conflicts to ensure that productivity does not get affected. In Chapter 8, we talked about the different types of conflict and gave you tools that will help you and your team.

Being a manager entails implementing your organization's strategic plan at a departmental level. It is therefore imperative that you familiarize yourself with your organization's business strategies, goals, and the actions needed to achieve those goals. This will empower you to communicate effectively with your team when implementing the strategy at a departmental level. Additionally, this information will help you when setting your KPIs.

For an organization to grow, it needs to embrace change. However, if change is not properly communicated, it will cause discord and distress in the workforce. Managers have to be prepared to help their team members during such periods of transition, and sometimes confusion.

Finally, the truth is, your first year as a manager will be difficult, but keep in mind that things will get easier and more familiar.

CONCLUSION

The best way to excel in your new role is to take every learning opportunity presented to you. Learn from other managers, seek a mentor, ask questions, and listen more than you talk. Above all, take every task in your stride, and remember: Tomorrow is another opportunity to get things right.

# REFERENCES

AEU LEAD. (2021, March 22). *Five self-management skills every manager should master*. Default. https://www.aeulead.com/main-navigation/insights/article/five-self-management-skills-every-manager-should-master

Baril, M. (2016, February 11). *9 early warning signs of workplace conflict*. Resologics. https://www.resologics.com/resologics-blog/2016/1/8/9-early-warning-signs-of-workplace-conflict

Bourke, J., & Dillon, B. (2018). The diversity and inclusion revolution Eight powerful truths. https://www2.deloitte.com/content/dam/insights/us/articles/4209_Diversity-and-inclusion-revolution/DI_Diversity-and-inclusion-revolution.pdf

Borysenko, K. (2019, January 5). *Ten things new managers need to know*. Forbes. https://www.forbes.com/sites/karlynborysenko/2019/01/04/ten-things-new-managers-need-to-know/

Bourke, J., & Titus, A. (2019, March 29). *Why inclusive leaders are good for organizations, and how to become one*. Harvard Business Review. https://hbr.org/2019/03/why-inclusive-leaders-are-good-for-organizations-and-how-to-become-one

Brownstone, K., & Fagan-Smith, B. (2021, April 8). *4 causes of workplace conflicts*. ROI. https://roico.com/2021/04/08/4-causes-of-workplace-conflict/

Burgers, C., Eden, A., van Engelenburg, M. D., & Buningh, S. (2015). How feedback boosts motivation and play in a brain-training game. *Computers in Human Behavior, 48*, 94–103. https://doi.org/10.1016/j.chb.2015.01.038

CFI. (2018). *Strategic planning - Definition, steps, and benefits*. Corporate Finance Institute. https://corporatefinanceinstitute.com/resources/knowledge/strategy/strategic-planning/

# REFERENCES

Clear Review. (2019). *How to write clear SMART objectives with employees.* Clear Review. https://www.clearreview.com/resources/guides/get-employees-write-clear-motivational-smart-objectives

Coco, V. (2021, September 30). *3 Reasons purpose-driven leadership is important in the workplace.* Www.cococonsulting.ch. https://www.cococonsulting.ch/blog/3-reasons-purpose-driven-leadership-is-important-in-the-workplace

Compass Office. (2022). *Brands with purpose: 5 purpose-led companies to watch in 2022.* Compassoffices.com. https://www.compassoffices.com/en/about-us/blogs/brands-with-purpose-5-purpose-led-companies-to-watch-in-2022/

Council, F. C. (2018, May 23). *15 change management mistakes you're probably making.* Forbes. https://www.forbes.com/sites/forbescoachescouncil/2018/05/23/15-change-management-mistakes-youre-probably-making/

Deloitte. (2018). 2018 Deloitte Millennial Survey Millennials. In *Deloitte.* https://www2.deloitte.com/content/dam/Deloitte/global/Documents/About-Deloitte/gx-2018-millennial-survey-report.pdf

Dhingra, N., Samo, A., Schaninger, B., & Schrimper, M. (2021, April 5). *Help your employees find purpose--or watch them leave | McKinsey.* Www.mckinsey.com. https://www.mckinsey.com/business-functions/people-and-organizational-performance/our-insights/help-your-employees-find-purpose-or-watch-them-leave

Engagedly. (2021, March 29). *7 common goal setting mistakes managers should avoid.* Engagedly. https://engagedly.com/7-common-goal-setting-mistakes-managers-should-avoid/

Forbes. (n.d.). *Walt Disney (DIS).* Forbes. https://www.forbes.com/companies/walt-disney/

Granish, J. (n.d.). *The ultimate list of delegation dos and don'ts.* https://www.alpinesbsolutions.com/delegation-dos-and-donts-va/

# REFERENCES

Grossmann, C. (2021, April 21). *How to Inspire Employees and Give a Sense of Purpose | Beekeeper*. Https://Www.beekeeper.io/. https://www.beekeeper.io/blog/3-inspiring-ways-give-employees-sense-purpose/

Home Business Mag. (2022). *What you need to know about setting goals as a first-time manager*. Homebusinessmag.com. https://homebusinessmag.com/management/how-to-guides-management/need-know-setting-goals-first-time-manager/

Hunt, V., Layton, D., & Prince, S. (2015b, January 1). *Why diversity matters*. Www.mckinsey.com. https://www.mckinsey.com/business-functions/people-and-organizational-performance/our-insights/why-diversity-matters

Indeed Editorial Team. (2020, November 27). *4 levels of conflict and tips for managing them | Indeed.com*. Www.indeed.com. https://www.indeed.com/career-advice/career-development/levels-of-conflict

Indeed Editorial Team. (2021a, March 7). *Your guide to successful delegation and team management | Indeed.com*. Indeed Career Guide. https://www.indeed.com/career-advice/career-development/guide-successful-delegation-team-management

Indeed Editorial Team. (2021b, March 8). *Delegation types and skills*. Indeed Career Guide. https://www.indeed.com/career-advice/career-development/delegation-examples

Indeed Editorial Team. (2021c, August 20). *7 Steps of the strategic planning process*. Indeed Career Guide. https://www.indeed.com/career-advice/career-development/strategic-planning-process

Indeed Editorial Team. (2021d, November 2). *14 tips for managing people at work*. Indeed Career Guide. https://www.indeed.com/career-advice/career-development/managing-people

Indeed Editorial Team. (2021e, November 4). *Management styles: overview and examples*. Www.indeed.com. https://www.indeed.com/career-advice/career-development/management-styles

# REFERENCES

Kerfoot, K. (1998). Management is taught, leadership is learned. *Plastic Surgical Nursing, 18*(2), 108–109. https://doi.org/10.1097/00006527-199818020-00010

Kuligowski, K. (2021, November 19). *How to be a diverse and inclusive company.* Business News Daily. https://www.businessnewsdaily.com/15970-diverse-inclusive-companies.html

Landry, L. (2018, November 29). *9 mistakes to avoid as a first-time manager.* Business Insights - Blog. https://online.hbs.edu/blog/post/first-time-manager-tips

Lester, S. W., & Brower, H. H. (2003). In the Eyes of the Beholder: The Relationship Between Subordinates' Felt Trustworthiness and their Work Attitudes and Behaviors. *Journal of Leadership & Organizational Studies, 10*(2), 17–33. https://doi.org/10.1177/107179190301000203

Libby, A. (n.d.). *First-time manager? How to fast-track your education.* The Muse. https://www.themuse.com/advice/firsttime-manager-how-to-fasttrack-your-education

Lorenzo, R. (2020, July 17). *How diverse leadership teams boost innovation.* BCG Global. https://www.bcg.com/publications/2018/how-diverse-leadership-teams-boost-innovation

Miller, K. (2020). *A manager's guide to successful strategy implementation | HBS Online.* Business Insights - Blog. https://online.hbs.edu/blog/post/strategy-implementation-for-managers

Murray, A. S. (2010). *The Wall Street journal essential guide to management: Lasting lessons from the best leadership minds of our time.* Harper Business.

Owens, A. (2019, May 21). *10 characteristics of an effective manager.* AdviserPlus. https://adviserplus.com/insights/10-characteristics-of-an-effective-manager/

PrincePerelson. (2019, December 16). *The importance of diversity in the workplace.* PrincePerelson & Associates. https://perelson.com/the-importance-of-diversity-in-the-workplace/

# REFERENCES

Reddy, C. (2016, February 7). *How to lead with purpose: 9 simple and best ways.* WiseStep. https://content.wisestep.com/lead-with-purpose/

Runrun.it. (2019, October 22). *The many challenges of a first time manager and how to address them.* Runrun.it Blog. https://blog.runrun.it/en/first-time-manager/

Shekeryk, N. (2021, August 4). *5 ways managers can help employees find a sense of purpose in the workplace.* Limeade. https://www.limeade.com/resources/blog/help-employees-find-a-sense-of-purpose-in-the-workplace

Shonk, K. (2019, April 23). *What is conflict resolution, and how does it work?* PON - Program on Negotiation at Harvard Law School. https://www.pon.harvard.edu/daily/conflict-resolution/what-is-conflict-resolution-and-how-does-it-work/

van der Hoek, M., Groeneveld, S., & Kuipers, B. (2016). Goal setting in teams: Goal clarity and team performance in the public sector. *Review of Public Personnel Administration, 38*(4), 472–493. https://doi.org/10.1177/0734371x16682815

# ABOUT THE AUTHOR

Celeste is a Nurse Manager in the North West of the United Kingdom with over 15 years experience in the field. She studied Pharmacology at The University of Manchester, followed by Adults Nursing Diploma at Manchester Metropolitan University. After that, just to the mix, she graduated as a Community Specialist Practitioner at the University of Bolton.

Celeste's been married for 24 years and a proud mother to four children, three of whom are teenagers and one young adult daughter who has just graduated from University of the Arts London. But she is also a former Basketball player, and Bookseller.

Celeste is a leading member in her community and has been an inspiration to others who have followed her footsteps.

CPSIA information can be obtained
at www.ICGtesting.com
Printed in the USA
BVHW021232191122
652278BV00028B/2725